THE BOOTSTRAPPER'S BIBLE

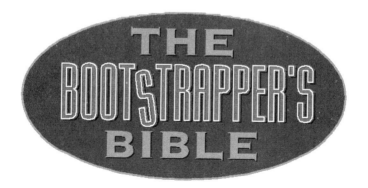

How to Start and Build a Business with a Great Idea and (Almost) No Money

Seth Godin

Upstart
Publishing Company®
Specializing in Small Business Publishing
a division of Dearborn Publishing Group, Inc.

Acquisitions Editor: Danielle Egan-Miller
Managing Editor: Jack Kiburz
Interior Design: Seth Godin Productions, Inc.
Cover Design: Design Alliance, Inc.

© 1998 by Seth Godin Productions, Inc.

Published by Upstart Publishing Company®,
a division of Dearborn Publishing Group, Inc.

Printed in the United States of America
98 99 00   10 9 8 7 6 5 4 3 2 1

Library of Congress Cataloging-in-Publication Data
Godin, Seth
         The bootstrapper's bible : how to start and build a business with a great
    idea and (almost) no money / Seth Godin.
                   p.   cm.
         Includes index.
         ISBN 1-57410-103-X (pbk.)
         1. New business enterprises. 2. Small business. I. Title.
    HD62.5.G632   1998
    658.1'141--dc21   98-28293
                                                                        CIP

Upstart books are available at special quantity discounts to use as premiums and sales promotions, or for use in corporate training programs. For more information, please call the Special Sales Manager at 800-621-9621, ext. 4394, or write to Dearborn Financial Publishing, Inc., 155 North Wacker Drive, Chicago, IL, 60606-1719.

dedicated to my wife, Helene

Acknowledgments

Too many people have helped me write this book. I've been bootstrapping since I started my first business in 1972, at the age of 12. If I tried to thank every patient teacher, every inspiring mentor, every hardworking employee, every flexible vendor and customer, I'd never get on with writing the book. But I do want to thank Mark Henricks for writing up all those great bootstrapper profiles.

So, if you're reading this and you belong in this section of the book, please, please, please insert your name here and know that you have my gratitude and appreciation. If life is a journey, this has been one hell of a ride so far…and I'm enjoying every minute of it. Thanks.

Contents

INTRODUCTION

No one in this country has the right to a job.

Every American, on the other hand, has the right to start his own business.

Think about that for a second. No license required, no governmental approval of any kind. If you've got something of value to sell, you can start your own company and go ahead and do it. Is this a great country, or what?

This is a book about starting with little capital and achieving that American dream. About accomplishing more than you ever thought possible—creating a great job, a terrific lifestyle, a chance to make a lot of money while providing products and services that make the economy work better.

Virtually every business was boot- strapped

In 1903, a 24-year-old Hungarian immigrant named William Fuchs saw his first motion picture. The uneducated garment worker was so enamored of the pictures crudely projected on the wall of a New York City candy store that he committed his life savings— the princely sum of $1,700—to open a 146-seat theater in Brooklyn. Not a grand beginning, agreed?

Obviously, 1903 was quite a while ago. But let's make a long story short. Fuchs changed his last name to Fox. And that theater was the forebear of Twentieth Century–Fox, the Fox Television Network, Fox Sports Network, and, probably, quite a few more entertainment businesses to come.

A bootstrapper starts with virtually no money, lots of inspiration, and plenty of hard work. Pulling on his own bootstraps, he turns that sweat into a business that survives, that thrives, that adds value for its customers and creates salary and satisfaction for its employees.

Bootstrappers built this country, and they continue to make it great. Virtually every business—from IBM to the local dry cleaner—was bootstrapped, usually by people with far less smarts, less money, fewer connections, and less vision than you have right now.

Being a bootstrapper is about freedom. The freedom to make your choices, to answer to no one but your customers, to carve out a piece of the world and make it yours.

For most entrepreneurs, recapturing the energy and excitement of their first years as a bootstrapper remains an elusive goal. The thrill of forging ahead when you've got nothing to lose—the opportunity to prove the critics wrong, to start at zero and build—is something you get to have only once.

I've been there. In 1986, I bootstrapped my first company. Today, I employ more than 40 people and we'll probably generate more than $5 million in revenue this year. Along the way, I've also been privileged to receive more than $4 million in venture money, so I know what the process looks like from the other side. I've dealt with bankers and business plans and key man insurance and fancy dinners—mere weeks after recycling paper clips to save a few bucks.

Believe it or not, bootstrapping can often be better. Boostrappers can focus on their agenda all the time. And if you structure your business properly, you can even make a lot of money. I wouldn't recommend starting out any other way. Bootstrapping teaches entrepreneurs lessons they will never learn if they start with money. It forces you to be creative, flexible, resourceful. Most of all, it forces you to listen to the market, instead of having the hubris to tell the market what you think it needs to hear.

The world is littered with businesses that blew $5 million, $10 million, even $100 million of other people's money in search of the big idea. In this book, I'm going to examine companies that were started on less than a year's pay. Lots and lots of them are household names.

But bootstrapping isn't just about building the next billion-dollar business. More often than not, it's about building a small but profitable business, a good living, a good lifestyle, and control over what you do. It's a dream that's within the reach of anyone who reads this book.

In these pages you'll reap the advice of hundreds of entrepreneurs who boot-strapped their businesses. You'll find out about marketing and sales and finance and manufacturing and positioning and public relations and hiring and equity—and how to balance the monkey on your back (your business) with the rest of your life.

If this book has one goal, it's this: to make you understand that if we did it, you can do it, too. The worst thing isn't failing. It's not trying in the first place.

What happened to Dineh Mohajer is what every bootstrapper dreams of. Walking through the mall while wearing her own hand-mixed shade of nail polish, the 22-year-old USC premed student kept getting buttonholed by people who wanted to know where she'd bought it. Backed by $200, she mixed up a few samples. While she was pitching them to a buyer at an expensive boutique, a teenager rushed up and bought all she had, at $18 a bottle. The buyer ordered 200 bottles on the spot, and Mohajer's company, which she called Hard Candy, was on its way.

Nine months later, Hard Candy was on the way to doing $10 million a year—and the founder was on the way to exhaustion. Wrung out from the unfamiliar demands of managing a business experiencing explosive growth, Mohajer stopped eating, sleeping, or caring whether her bootstrap broke even or went broke. Her response: hire a professional manager to tackle the mundane details of running a start-up, while she concentrated on coming up with new nail polishes. Today Hard Candy polishes are in stores from Nordstrom's to Bloomingdale's, and the founder is finding a way to be a successful bootstrapper and a successful human being.

Balance the monkey on your back (your business) with the rest of your life

Boot- strappers can focus on their agenda all the time

When Jake Burton started selling snowboards, almost nobody had ever heard of the sport. He had to scrape to buy awareness-building ads before even hard-core snow-sport fans had any idea snowboarding existed. That was in 1977. Today snowboarding is an Olympic event, splashed across TV screens around the globe. But Burton Snowboards, of Burlington, Vermont, still focuses on snowboarding as a sport and not as a mass culture trend.

The apparel Burton sells is for snowboarding— not for the street chic. "That's not who we're going after," he explains. Bootstrappers who risk it all in an effort to appeal to a broader base than they can support are heading for trouble, he warns. If Burton sounds entirely too cautious for a sport with a let-it-all-hang-out image, consider that Burton Snowboards is older than some of the people who competed in Nagano. If he says a slope is too steep to go down, it probably is.

When Chuck Miller listens, his customers talk. The owner of Aztec Tents & Events in Torrance, California, routinely sends out survey forms to customers of his party-equipment rental firm. He wants to know everything from how the employees behaved to the quality of the equipment. And when responses are bad, Miller personally calls to get more details.

The attention to the marketplace has helped this bootstrapper fine-tune his offerings. But more important, it encourages people to call him and let him know what they want. And when he personally phones for more info, it floors people. As a result, he gets back an amazing 80 percent of the surveys, each loaded with information and worth its weight in gold.

Boot-strapping forces you to listen to the market

CHAPTER ONE

WELCOME
TO THE
BOOTSTRAP
WORLD

W hat's a bootstrapper?

Well, since you bought this book, chances are that you qualify! For me, a bootstrapper isn't someone who fits a particular demographic or even someone in a certain financial situation. Instead, bootstrapping is a state of mind.

Bootstrappers run billion-dollar companies, nonprofit organizations, and start-ups in their basements. A bootstrapper is determined to build a business that pays for itself every day. In many ways, it's easiest to define a bootstrapper by what she isn't: a money-raising bureaucrat who specializes in using other people's money to take big risks in growing a business. Not that there's anything wrong with that...

You can use the information in this book to make any company more focused, more efficient, and more grassroots. Throughout this book, though, I'll be primarily addressing classic bootstrappers: entrepreneurs who are working their butts off to start a great business from scratch with no (or almost no) money.

At last count, there were several million bootstrappers in this country, with another few million wannabes just waiting for the opportunity. My goal is to give you enough insight and confidence that you'll get off the bench and make it happen.

THE BOOTSTRAPPER'S MANIFESTO

Tape this to your bathroom mirror and read it out loud every night before you go to bed:

I am a bootstrapper. I have initiative and insight and guts, but not much money. I will succeed because my efforts and my focus will defeat bigger and better-funded competitors. I am fearless. I keep my focus on growing the business—not on politics, career advancement, or other wasteful distractions.

I will leverage my skills to become the key to every department of my company, yet realize that hiring experts can be the secret to my success. I will be a fervent and intelligent user of technology, to conserve my two most precious assets: time and money.

My secret weapon is knowing how to cut through bureaucracy. My size makes me faster and more nimble than any company could ever be.

I am a laser beam. Opportunities will try to cloud my focus, but I will not waver from my stated goal and plan—until *I* change it. And I know that plans were made to be changed.

I'm in it for the long haul. Building a business that will *last* separates me from the opportunist, and is an investment in my brand and my future. Surviving is succeeding, and each day that goes by makes it easier still for me to reach my goals.

Happy with small fish

A guide to Japanese sword fighting? The definitive guide to falconry? Reissued adventures of Freddie the Pig? These aren't the kinds of books that tooted Peter Mayer's flute when he was the CEO of the giant publisher Penguin Books. But they're the lifeblood of Overlook Press, a $3 million micro-publisher he started and then left over 20 years ago. Now those books are music to Mayer's ears.

"Unusual titles in obscure areas" could describe the output of Overlook since Mayer's return. Why? He seeks the oddball and the overlooked. And he knows they may escape the radar of the likes of Penguin, but they're well within his purview. Among Overlook's successes has been a long- and strong-selling book that House Speaker Newt Gingrich read, loved, and proclaimed a must-read for his staff: *The Book of Five Rings*—sword-fighting guide.

Access to capital

As the former CEO of Lotus Development Corporation, Jim Manzi clearly knew how to run a high-tech company. So when he left Lotus to take up the reins at the Internet business-to-business catalog seller Nets, Inc., everybody expected great things.

Manzi succeeded in setting up mergers that seriously drained the company's resources of management, time, and money. Worse, he had no knack for the crucial task of raising money to keep things going. While Lotus had been able simply to sell stock to fund expensive projects such as the development of new versions of 1-2-3, Nets, Inc., simply ran through its venture capital funding and was left high and dry. Nets, Inc., filed for Chapter 11 bankruptcy protection within two years, and Manzi was out on his ear. Score another one for access to capital.

I pledge to know more about my field than anyone else. I will read and learn and teach. My greatest asset is the value I can add to my clients through my efforts.

I realize that treating people well on the way up will make it nicer for me on the way back down. I will be scrupulously honest and direct in my dealings, and won't use my position as a fearless bootstrapper to gain unfair advantage. My reputation will follow me wherever I go, and I will invest in it daily and protect it fiercely.

I am the underdog. I realize that others are rooting for me to succeed, and I will gratefully accept their help when offered. I also understand the power of favors, and will offer them and grant them whenever I can.

I have less to lose than most—a fact I can turn into a significant competitive advantage.

I am a salesperson. Sooner or later, my income will depend on sales, and those sales can be made only by me, not by an emissary, not by a rep. I will sell by helping others get what they want, by identifying needs and filling them.

I am a guerrilla. I will be persistent, consistent, and willing to invest in the marketing of myself and my business.

I will measure what I do, and won't lie about it to myself or my spouse. I will set strict financial goals and honestly evaluate my performance. I'll set limits on time and money and won't exceed either.

Most of all, I'll remember that the journey is the reward. I will learn and grow and enjoy every single day.

TRUE STORY 1: I AM A LASER BEAM

The big call came just a few months after Michael Joaquin Grey and Matthew Brown had started up their toy company. Would the two San Francisco bootstrappers like their product included in the movie marketing blitz for *The Lost World*? Nope, said Grey and Brown, who preferred to stick with their vision of gradually building a market for Zoob, their plastic DNA-like building toy.

What the bootstrappers feared was a loss of identity. If they hooked up with the celluloid dinosaurs, they'd be seen as just another *Jurassic* spinoff. On their own, they could create a separate brand and not only avoid extinction but create their own world. Eventually, the two even hope to have their own Zoob movies.

TRUE STORY 2: THE BOOTSTRAPPER IS HERE FOR THE LONG HAUL

Jheri Redding started not one, but four companies. And when the renowned bootstrapper died at 91 in 1998, all four—including the first, Jheri Redding Products, begun in 1956—were still in operation. How'd he do it?

Redding created lasting businesses through the combination of a gift for spotting long-term opportunity and his relentless drive to create significant competitive advantages in product features and distribution clout. The Illinois farm boy became a cosmetologist during the Great Depression because he saw hairdressers prospering and farmers failing. He soon began experimenting with shampoo formulas and showed remarkable flair for innovation.

Redding was the first to add vitamins and minerals to shampoos, the first to balance the acidity of the formulas, and the first to urge hairdressers to supplement their haircutting income by selling his products on the slow days of Monday, Tuesday, and Wednesday. The first? Yes, and also the last. There aren't many like Jheri Redding, who also founded Redken (1960), Jhirmack (1976), and Nexxus Products (1979).

TRUE STORY 3: I WILL KNOW MORE ABOUT MY FIELD THAN ANYONE ELSE

When Yves Chouinard starting scaling mountains, rock climbers used soft cast-iron pitons that had to be discarded after a single use. Chouinard, who was as passionate about climbing peaks as he was about his work as a blacksmith, designed a new piton of aircraft-quality chrome-molybdenum steel. The tougher, reusable piton met climbers' needs much better and became an instant success.

As piton sales climbed, Chouinard himself kept climbing too, as much as or more than ever. He recalls, "Every time I returned from the mountains, my head was spinning with ideas for improving the carabiners, crampons, ice axes, and other tools of climbing."

It's been 40 years since the blacksmith-climber hammered out his first steel piton. Since then, it and his many other designs have become the foundation for Patagonia, Inc., a $100 million outdoor apparel company based in Ventura, California. Although he's now a highly successful businessman, Chouinard still climbs regularly, testing his company's new products while honing its most important tool: his own matchless knowledge of climbers' needs.

TRUE STORY 4: I AM A SALESPERSON

Shereé Thomas had a personal question in mind when she called the customer service line of the company that makes Breathe Right nasal strips. But when she found herself talking to the company's medical director, she went beyond her question and revved up a sales pitch for a liquid she had invented that neutralizes the smell of cigarette smoke on clothes and hair.

A couple of switchboard clicks later, Thomas was on the line with the company's president. And three weeks after that, the company had signed a licensing agreement to invest $4 million to manufacture, market, and distribute Banish, the product Thomas mixed up in her chemist-grandfather's garage. Through the licensing deal, this Cedar Park, Texas, bootstrapper will rack up around six figures

ABYSSBOOKS

Brand equity

When Pete Fratus launched his online bookstore back in 1991, the Bastrop, Texas, entrepreneur had the whole Internet largely to himself. Starting with $20,000 and working out of a warehouse behind their home, he and his wife, Maria Muñoz, built AbyssBooks into a solid company that by 1995 was doing $850,000 a year selling mostly technical books over the Net.

Then came Amazon.com. The brainchild of financial expert Jeff Bezos raised millions of dollars in capital, which it plowed into building name recognition. AbyssBooks was soon relegated to also-ran status in the World Wide Web book-selling derby. Revenues halved, then fell further, while online ad costs went up 30-fold. By 1998, AbyssBooks had stopped selling books on its own and primarily acted to funnel buyers to the Web site that had become the name brand for online book buying—Amazon.com. And even though Fratus got there first, he finished last, because the bigger company had a stronger brand.

Go where the other guys can't

Ani DiFranco gets buyout offers all the time from big record companies. But why should she take them? Ten years ago, the then-teenaged Buffalo, New York, folksinger borrowed $1,500 to make a demo tape. After selling 300 copies, DiFranco started Righteous Babe Records and today has sold 1.5 million albums of her songs.

DiFranco has done it by doing what mainstream record companies can't. First of all, she's raw. Her songs are about her failed relationships, her abortion, the roughest ends of her nerves. Audiences love that. Her business partners love the punky singer's smooth side. This bootstrapper is an ideal customer, supplier, and friend. She records her albums in Buffalo, has them pressed in Buffalo, and even prints T-shirts and liner notes in Buffalo—though she could get everything done more cheaply elsewhere. And she sends her business her friends' way: her manager, CD manufacturer, and T-shirt printer have all been with her since before she was famous.

Could a big record company do it that way? There's not enough money to convince Ani DiFranco they could.

in annual royalty payments. Her investment in the sale: a phone call to the company's toll-free line—and a personal commitment never to stop selling.

TRUE STORY 5: THE JOURNEY IS THE REWARD

Charles Foley was 18 when he told his mother he expected to invent things that would be used everywhere. At 67, the inventor has 130 patents to his credit, including one for the venerable party game Twister, which he invented in the 1960s and which still sells today.

But Foley, of Charlotte, North Carolina, is still at the inventing game. He recently revived a discovery of his from the 1960s, an adhesive-removing liquid, and sold the rights to make and market it to a company headed by his son. He's also working on new designs for fishing floats and a home security system.

Driven to search for success? Hardly. Foley's just following his bootstrapping nature on a journey that's lasted a lifetime. "I was born with a gift," he says with a shrug. "Ideas pop into my head."

WHAT'S A BIG COMPANY GOT THAT YOU HAVEN'T GOT?

Most of the companies you deal with every day, read about in the media, or learn about in school are companies with hundreds or thousands of employees. They have an ongoing cash flow and a proven business model. (I'll explain what that is in the next chapter.)

Because this is the way you've always seen business done, it's easy to imagine that the *only* way to run a business is with secretaries and annual reports and lawyers and fancy offices. Of course, this isn't true, but it's worth taking a look at the important distinctions between what *they* do and what *you* do.

Just as playing table tennis is very different from playing Wimbledon tennis, bootstrapping your own business is a world apart from running IBM. You need to understand the differences, and you need to understand how you can use your size to your advantage.

Traditional companies succeed for a number of reasons, but there are five key leverage points that many of them capitalize on.

1. *Distribution.* How is it that Random House publishes so many best-selling books, or Warner Music so many hit records? Distribution is at the heart of how most businesses that sell to consumers succeed. In a nutshell, if you can't get it in the store, it won't sell.

Companies with a lot of different products can afford to hire a lot of salespeople. They can spread their advertising across numerous products and they can offer retailers an efficient way to fill their stores with goods.

Traditional retailers want the companies that sell them products to take all the risks. They want guarantees that the products will sell. They want national advertising to drive consumers into the store. They insist on co-op money, in which the manufacturer pays them to advertise the product locally.

That's why Kellogg's cereals are consistently at the top of the market share list. Lots of smaller companies can make a better cereal, and they can certainly sell it for less. But Kellogg's is willing to pay a bribe (called a "shelving allowance") to get plenty of space at the supermarket. Kellogg's airs commercials during Saturday morning TV shows. And Kellogg's has hundreds of sales reps wandering the aisles of grocery stores around the country.

Kellogg's wins the market share battle in mass-market cereals because it succeeds at the last and most important step: getting the product in front of the consumer.

2. *Access to capital.* The big guys can borrow money. Lots of it. It's no big deal for a car company to raise $200 million to pay for a new line of cars. In industries where the expenses for machinery, tooling, research

and development, and marketing are high, big companies with cheap money often prevail.

Microsoft, for example, took six or more years to turn Windows from a lame excuse for a product into the market-busting operating system it is now. Year after year after year, it lost money marketing lousy versions of Windows. How could it afford to do this? By raising money from the stock market at very low cost and hanging in.

Big companies have access to capital that a little guy can't hope to match. A hot company like Yahoo! is able to raise money from the stock market with no personal guarantees, no interest payments, no downside risk. And it can raise a lot. More established companies can issue bonds or get lines of credit for billions of dollars. The banks and investors that back these companies aren't looking for a monthly or even a yearly return on their investment. Instead, they're focusing on building profits a decade from now. A bootstrapper could never afford to compete with this approach.

If a market can be bought with cash, a big company will do it.

3. *Brand equity.* Why would you be more likely to try a new line of clothes from Nike than from Joe's Sporting Goods Store? Because Nike has invested billions of dollars in building a brand name, and you've learned to trust that name. Nike can leverage its name when introducing new products.

Don't underestimate the power of the brand! *Financial World* magazine estimates that the Marlboro name and logo are worth more than $2 billion. Any tobacco manufacturer can make a similar cigarette. But only Philip Morris gets to extract the profit that comes from having more than 50 percent market share.

If the consumer of the product is likely to buy from an established brand name, the big company has a huge advantage.

Most companies that do market research into lis-
tener tastes for radio stations take four to six
weeks to do a job. That's why Larry Rosin and Joe
Lenski decided that their New Jersey bootstrap,
which they called Edison Media Research, would
turn reports around in two weeks or less.

It wasn't easy, of course, but Rosin and Lenski
were younger and hungrier than the competition.
And before long, they were busier, too. In the
need-it-yesterday atmosphere of broadcasting, Edison found its rush-job focus provided compelling
benefits to media customers. And soon Edison was
one of the fastest-growing media research firms in
the country, with billings of more than $2 million
and customers like Sony and Time Warner.

Now, Lenski is turning his polling obsession to politics. He does exit polls and telephone interviews to
predict the outcome of political races, then peddles the
information to news organizations anxious to be first
to report projected wins and losses. The next time
you're awed by a CNN anchor's ability to pick a winner hours before the polls close or wonder why your
favorite DJ played a catchy-sounding record once and
then never again, blame it on Edison—and speed.

Small, focused teams are always faster

4. *Customer relationships*. Especially for companies that sell in the business-to-business world, access to customers is a tremendous advantage. Time Warner collects nearly one-third of all the advertising dollars spent on magazines in this country every year. When Time launches a new magazine, it has a tremendous advantage in selling the ad space. A fledgling competitor, on the other hand, has to start from scratch.

Last year, Costco sold more than $30 million worth of shrimp in its giant warehouse stores. The company can choose from hundreds of different shrimp suppliers (it all comes from the same ocean!), but it deals with only three firms. Why? Because the shrimp buyer at Costco doesn't have time to sift through every possible supplier every time she makes a new purchase. So she works with companies she trusts, companies she's worked with before.

In established markets, customer relationships are a huge advantage.

5. *Great employees*. Big companies are filled with turkeys, lifers, incompetents, and political operators. But there, among the bureaucrats, are some exceptional people. Great inventors, designers, marketers, salespeople, customer service wizards, and manufacturers. These great people are drawn to a company that has a great reputation, offers stability, and pays well. Smart companies like Disney leverage these people to the hilt.

During a meeting with someone at Disney, I saw a stack of paper on the corner of his desk. "What's that?" I asked. He replied that they were résumés. More than 200 of them, all from extraordinarily qualified people, one with a gorgeous watercolor on it. All of them had come from one tiny classified ad in the LA paper. Big companies attract powerfully talented people.

What's a bootstrapper to do? Big companies have better distribution, access to money whenever it's needed, a brand that customers trust, access to the people who buy, and great employees. They've got lots of competition, big and small, and they've sharpened their axes for battle. Do you have a chance to succeed?

No.

Not if you try to compete head to head in these five areas. Not if you try to be just like a big company, but smaller. If you try to steal the giant's lunch, the giant is likely to eat *you* for lunch.

Inventing a new computer game and trying to sell it in retail outlets would be crazy—Electronic Arts and Broderbund will cream you. Introducing a new line of sneakers to compete head to head with Nike at the core of its market would be suicidal.

You have to go where the other guys can't. Take advantage of what you have so that you can beat the competition with what they don't have.

Many bootstrappers miss this lesson. They believe that great ideas and lots of energy will always triumph, so they waste countless dollars and years fighting the bad guys on their own turf.

That's why the gourmet food business bugs me so much. Every year, another 2,000 gourmet items—jams, jellies, nuts, spreads, chips—are introduced. And every year, 1,900 of them fail. Why? Because the bootstrappers behind them are in love with an idea, not a business. Successful bootstrappers know that just because they can make a product doesn't mean they should. Making kettle-fried potato chips from your grandmother's recipe may sound appealing, but that doesn't mean that you can grow the idea into a real business.

Given the choice between building a thriving, profitable business with a niche and a really boring product and putting your life savings into an intensely competitive business where you're likely to fail but the product is cool, the experienced bootstrapper will pick the former every time. If you find an industry filled with wannabe entrepreneurs with a dollar and a dream, run away and look for something else!

Now let's take a look at the good news. You have plenty of things that the big guys don't, things that can give you tremendous advantages in launching a new business.

1. *Nothing to lose.* This is huge. Your biggest advantage. Big, established companies are in love with old, established ways. They have employees with a huge stake in maintaining the status quo. How many of the great railroad companies got into the airline business? Zero. Even though they could have completely owned this new mode of transport, they were too busy protecting their old turf to grab new turf.

Whenever a market or a technology changes, there's a huge opportunity for new businesses. The number one Web site on the Internet isn't run by Ziff Davis or Microsoft. It's run by an upstart bootstrapper named Jerry Yang (Yahoo!).

Fifteen years ago, I met with Jim Levy. At the time, he was running the fastest-growing company in the history of the world. Activision had exploded on the scene, introducing one video game after another, capturing a huge share of the Atari 2600 marketplace. After just one year, the company had transformed itself from bootstrapper to fat, happy bureaucracy.

As a freshly minted, slightly arrogant MBA, I decided it was my job to tell him what to do next. So I handed him an article from the *Harvard Business Review* and explained that he ought to start using some of the huge profits that Activision was earning to take over the brand-new software market. By making software for the IBM PC and Apple Macintosh, he could leverage his early lead and his cash and own even more markets.

But Jim had something to lose. His investors and his employees wanted more years like the one they'd just finished. They didn't want to hear about investing in new markets. They wanted to hear about profits. So Activision did more of the same.

A few years later, they were bought for, like, $4.34.

2. *Happy with small fish.* In the ocean, the first animals to die are the big fish. That's because they need to eat a lot to be happy. The small guys, the plankton, can make do with crumbs. Same is true with you. Disney can't be happy with a movie that earns less than $40 million at the box office. Compare this to the entrepreneur in Vermont who made a kids' video in 1990 called *Road Construction Ahead.* He was just delighted when he made more than $100,000.

Think about the orders of magnitude at work here: $40 million at the box office is 400 times $100,000. Just imagine all the room there is for a small business that operates under the radar of the giant.

Find a niche, not a nation.

3. *Presidential input.* In many companies, the president has no trouble getting things done. When Jack Welch at General Electric wants the ice maker on the new fridge to be quieter, you can bet people in the engineering department pay attention. And when Jack wants to have a meeting with some key customers in Detroit, odds are that they'll make time for him—hey, he's the president of the whole company.

But in big companies, the president is far removed from the action. GE has tens of thousands of employees and only one Jack Welch. He's surrounded by people with their own agendas. He rarely gets to change the whole company.

The other day, one of my employees flew to Detroit. He had a special-fare ticket and knew that his travel options might be restricted, but he got to the airport four hours early for his flight back. Another flight, virtually empty, was leaving in 15 minutes.

Jerry asked if he could fly standby. After all, the plane was flying back to New York anyway, it was empty, and it would cost the airline exactly zero to fly him back now, instead of four hours from now.

The gate agent said no. Do you think the president of the airline would have made the same decision? Do you think he would have wanted a valuable customer to spend four hours seething about the airline when he could have walked right onto a plane? Do you think the president would have wanted to see his valuable brand equity wasted in such a stupid way? I doubt it. But the president wasn't there. A gate agent having a bad day was there instead.

You, on the other hand, are the president of your company, and you have a lot of interaction with your customers. You make policy, so you'll never lose someone over a stupid rule. You can use this power and flexibility to make yourself irresistible to demanding customers.

4. *Rapid R&D.* As they say, you can't hire nine women to work really hard as a team and produce one baby in one month. Teamwork doesn't always make things faster—it can even slow them down.

Engineering studies have shown time and time again that small, focused teams are always faster than big, bureaucratic ones. Obviously, it's harder to pick a team of four great people than it is to assign two dozen randomly selected people to a project. And it's riskier, too. So most companies don't do very well when it comes to inventing breakthrough products.

When they've got a problem at IBM, they assign a squadron to it. A squadron that sometimes creates bad ideas, like the PC Jr. Barnes & Noble didn't invent Amazon.com. One smart guy named Jeff Bezos did. Microsoft and IBM didn't invent the supercool Palm Pilot. A much smaller company called US Robotics bought an even smaller company that developed it. Motorola and GE didn't invent the modern radar detector. Cincinnati Microwave did.

WATER TALKIES

Bootstrappers don't get a lot smaller than 11-year-old Richie Stachowski. But that didn't keep him from having a big idea. While snorkeling on a family vacation in Hawaii, Richie grew frustrated about being unable to talk underwater.

Not one to merely blow bubbles, Richie had no sooner returned home to Moraga, California, than he began trying to come up with a gadget that would let him speak while underwater. His solution? Water Talkies, a megaphone adapted for underwater use that lets snorkelers talk to each other from as far away as 15 feet.

With help from his family, Richie bootstrapped a company to manufacture the invention. And, thanks to a decision by Toys R Us to stock Water Talkies in its superstores nationwide, the big idea from the little bootstrapper is thoroughly afloat.

Great new ideas come out of tiny companies

Big companies will almost always try to reduce invention risk by assigning a bureaucracy. You, on the other hand, can do it yourself. Or hire one person to do it. That's why you so often see great new ideas come out of tiny companies. They're faster and more focused.

5. *The underdog.* When Viacom or Microsoft or General Motors comes knocking, lots of smaller companies smell money. They know that the person they're meeting with doesn't own the company (that employee might be five or ten levels away from anyone with total profit responsibility) so they're inclined to charge more. After all, the big guys can afford it!

In addition to charging big companies full retail prices, smaller businesses are used to the hassles that big companies present. Purchase orders and layers of bureaucracy. Lawyers and insurance policies and more. So in order to deal with the big guys' inherent inefficiences, they have to plan ahead and build the related costs into their prices when dealing with the Viacoms, Microsofts, and GMs.

Big companies don't treat people very well sometimes, and people respond in kind. You, on the other hand, run a small company. So you can acquire the distribution rights to a video series for no money down. Or convince Mel Gibson to appear in your documentary for union scale. Or get your lawyer to work for nothing, for a while, just because you're doing good things.

6. *Low overhead.* You work out of your house, with a simple phone system, no business affairs department, very little insurance, no company car, and volunteer labor. If you can't make it *much* more cheaply than the big guys, you've either picked the wrong product (hey, don't go into the computer chip business!) or you're going about it the wrong way.

Even though big companies are big in scale, they still have to turn a profit on each and every product they sell, or face the consequences sooner or later. The guy who's losing money on every order shipped and trying to make it up in volume is in for a rude awakening.

By leveraging your smallness, you can often undercut bigger competitors, especially if the product or service you create doesn't require a lot of fancy machinery.

7. *Time*. The big companies don't have a lot of freedom in the way they deal with time. When you have to pay off the bankers every month, please the stock market, and grow according to schedule, there isn't always the flexibility to do things on the right schedule. Sometimes they've got to rush things, and other times they hold things back.

You, on the other hand, are a stealth marketer. No one is watching you. Sometimes, when it counts, you'll be ten times faster than the big guys. But when you can make a difference by taking your time, you will—and it'll show.

A REAL-LIFE EXAMPLE OF TAKING ADVANTAGE OF YOUR SIZE (OR, HOW ID SOFTWARE COMPLETELY REDEFINED THE COMPUTER GAME MARKET AND MADE MILLIONS)

The software company that calls itself id is a classic bootstrapper. It makes violent computer games that run on home computers. Its software is usually developed by a group of 2 to 10 people, then published by a big company like Electronic Arts. It costs a huge amount to make a new product (sometimes more than a million dollars) but amazingly little to make one more copy (as little as 50 cents).

So the idea in computer game software has always been to spend whatever it takes to make a great game, then spend whatever it takes to get shelf space in the software stores, then hope and pray that you sell a *lot* of copies. One hit like Myst can pay all of a company's bills for years to come.

Id became famous for a game called Castle Wolfenstein. As an encore, the four guys who founded id decided to follow their own rules in playing against the big companies. They did it with a game called Doom.

They brazenly broke the first rule of software marketing—they gave Doom away to anyone who wanted to download it. *Free.* Millions of people did. It quickly became the most popular computer game of the year. It didn't cost id very much to allow someone to download the game, but the company wasn't receiving any income at all.

In stage two, id offered a deluxe version of Doom with more levels, more monsters, more everything. Partnering with a big guy (GT Interactive), it got the software into stores around the country. And sold it directly by mail order.

With a user base of millions of people, id got to call the shots. Instead of being at the mercy of the gatekeepers of distribution, it was courted by distributors and retailers. By inventing a completely different business model, a model in which it had nothing to lose, id redefined a business and won.

Take a look at all the attributes listed in this chapter. Id took advantage of the seven that help the bootstrapper and steadfastly avoided the five that help the big company. By redefining the game and playing on its home field, it trounced companies valued at more than half a billion dollars.

Here's how id used the seven bootstrapper tools:

1. *Nothing to lose.* The method used by id threatened to destroy software distribution as we know it. Which was fine with id, but not so fine with the guys at the big software companies. There's no way in the world they would have had the guts to do this themselves.

2. *Happy with small fish.* Because id didn't spend any money on advertising, and because it had developed the game itself, it didn't need Doom to be the best-selling computer game of the year to be happy. Even 30,000 sales would have been enough to make the venture successful.

Rose Blumkin started the Nebraska Furniture Mart in an Omaha basement with $500 borrowed from her brother. She couldn't match her bigger competitors' selection, showrooms, or service. But she could survive on a much smaller profit margin. In fact, Blumkin said a 10 percent margin was ample for her. "Everybody else gets 40 or 50 percent," she once said. "It's too much!"

Actually, Blumkin turned out to be too much. Too much for her competitors, who tried to get her suppliers to blacklist her. Too much for some of her family members, differences with whom caused her to leave the company and start a next-door rival—at the age of 95! Too much, finally, even for the renowned investor Warren Buffett to resist: he paid $55 million to buy majority ownership in the Nebraska Furniture Mart in 1983. Today Blumkin's bootstrap boasts annual sales in excess of a quarter-billion dollars.

Undercut bigger competitors

BEN & JERRY'S

Position yourself against the brand leader

In 1980 Häagen-Dazs owned the superpremium ice cream market. The dessert, made in the Bronx and carrying a made-up name with no meaning in any language, was sold in all but three states and was garnering $30 million a year. This fact didn't escape would-be competitors, who flooded the market with fancy ice creams dubbed Frusen Glädjé, Alpen Zauber, and the like, most purportedly made in Switzerland, Sweden, or another cold-sounding place.

About the same time, Ben Cohen and Jerry Greenfield started selling handmade ice cream from a former gas station in Vermont. Instead of calling their product something foreign and exotic, however, they dubbed it Ben & Jerry's Homemade and made a point out of the fact that it was made by two real guys in Burlington. The ice cream was at least as good as every other superpremium brand, but the marketing position was exactly the opposite of everybody else's.

What happened? To consumers and retailers, the clones were just another Häagen-Dazs. And there was no room in anybody's freezer for more than one exotic superpremium. But there was room for a down-home, made-in-the-USA brand. Which is why Ben & Jerry's is now a $100 million company.

3. *Presidential input.* Id had total consistency. The game was designed, marketed, licensed, and managed by the same four people. No miscommunication here.

4. *Rapid R&D.* There were no budget committees, no marketing schedules, no organizational charts to get in the way. (It's interesting to note that it took three times as long for id to create Doom's sequel. The game's makers had apparently forgotten what they had learned about rapid R&D.)

5. *The underdog.* Consumers love to root for the hippies at id. It makes them more likely to spread the word and to buy (not copy) the final game.

6. *Low overhead.* There's no question that high overhead costs would have wiped these guys out.

7. *Time.* They knew they could ship when they needed to, instead of when shareholders demanded a new influx of sales. Because they controlled time, they could use it to their advantage.

The flip side of these seven attributes, of course, is what id *didn't* do. Here are some ways you can redefine the big guys out of the way on these five attributes:

1. *Distribution.* Never start by selling your product in major stores. Instead, use mail order. Or sell directly to just a few customers for lots of money per sale. Or use the Internet. The last step in your chain is traditional distribution.

2. *Access to capital.* Be cheap. In everything. Don't pick a business in which access to money is an important element. That means that building a cable service, a worldwide cellular phone system, or a chemical refinery probably wouldn't be on your list. When you do need capital, don't pay retail. Borrow from customers or suppliers.

Find an equity angel. But don't borrow at 18 percent! And don't use your personal credit cards.

3. *Brand equity.* Position yourself *against* the brand leader. Be "cheaper than Frito's" or "faster than Federal Express" or "cooler than Levi's." The more the other guy's brand gets publicized, the more your positioning statement increases in value. Be brazen in the way you compare yourself to the market leader. Your story should be short, solid, and memorable.

An alternative is to leverage an existing brand from a different category. Licensing the Fisher-Price name for a line of eyeglasses for kids, for example, helped one eyewear company decimate the competition. If one lives locally, consider tying in with a celebrity, a sports team, or a media partner. In each case you can use the very expensive brand equity that someone else has already built.

In chapter 8, I talk about developing a motto for your company and yourself. This is a great example of how that motto, that positioning statement, can pay off for you forever.

4. *Customer relationships.* You don't have much of a chance of grabbing a big piece of an established company's business away from one of its good customers. It's just too easy for the company to defend against you. Instead, you can try one of these strategies:

- The inchworm. Get a little piece of business as a test. Then, with great service and great products, slowly but surely steal more and more of the big guy's business. Focus on one client at a time. By the time the other guy catches on, it'll be too late.

- Sell to someone else. Either to companies that don't already have a relationship with your target customer or to someone in a different department at your target customer's company—someone who

The inchworm

In 1972, Herb Kelleher sketched out a triangle on the back of a cocktail napkin.

At the points of the triangle were three cities: Houston, Dallas, and San Antonio. It wasn't much of a business plan for a new airline, which was exactly the point. Kelleher figured by starting small he'd be able to serve these three Texas cities economically and profitably. Most important, he'd stay off the radar screens of American, United, and Delta, any one of which could easily crush him.

And that's just how it worked. Southwest Airlines became famous far beyond its route map for low prices and reliable, if no-frills, service. Gradually the airline expanded outside its first three cities to include other Texas destinations. Then it left the Lone Star State and eventually began flying coast to coast.

After 25 years, Southwest's Boeing 737s served 50 cities in 24 states with 2,200 flights daily and generated revenues of $3.4 billion. And it all started with a triangle on the back of a cocktail napkin.

Great employees

Every morning, Hyler Bracey slips five coins into one pant pocket. Each time the CEO of Atlanta Consulting Group praises one of his 46 employees, he takes a coin out of that pocket and puts it into another pocket.

At the end of the day, Bracey's empty pocket tells him whether he's done one of his most important jobs: motivating employees to stay on at a bootstrap when they could just as well be seeking higher pay and better benefits elsewhere.

doesn't know she's supposed to buy from any particular vendor. This strategy works at home, too. For example, Saturn found that by marketing its cars to women, it could grab market share that might have automatically gone to Ford if the car-buying decision for couples had been up to the man.

5. *Great employees*. Not every employee is searching for great reputation, stability, and high pay. Amazingly enough, there are lots of people who would prefer a great adventure, stock options, flextime, a caring boss, a convenient location, or a chance to grow without bureaucracy. By focusing on what *you* offer that the big guys don't, you can capture your own share of greatness.

This book, like most business books, may seem a little intimidating. It's filled with countless things you must do right and countless things that can go wrong.

In fact, you may feel like giving up.

And I can guarantee that if you don't feel like giving up today, there will definitely be days when you *do* feel like giving up. Which brings me to the most important, most concrete, most useful piece of advice in the whole book. Simple, but indispensable: *Don't give up*.

Surviving is succeeding. You're smarter than most people who have started their own businesses, and smarter still than those who have succeeded. It's not about what you know or even, in the end, about what you do. Success is persistence. Set realistic expectations. Don't give up.

You can't win if you're not in the game.

A lot of this book is about survival. A true bootstrapper worries about survival all the time. Why? Because if you fail, it's back to company cubicles, to work for someone else until you can get enough scratch together to try again.

Bootstrapping isn't always rational. For some of us (like me), it's almost an addiction. The excitement and sheer thrill of building something overwhelms the desire to play it safe. This is a book about how to make the odds work in your favor, how to keep playing until you win.

Great employees

Consumers know Starbucks as the fast-growing coffee bar chain. But it's more than that to employees of CEO Howard Schultz, who bootstrapped his first coffee bar in 1985 after seeing one seemingly on every corner in Milan, Italy. To them, Starbucks is perhaps the best retail job going. In fact, the Seattle company's turnover rate is about a fifth the national retail average.

Schultz explains the loyalty as a function of lots of training, plenty of respect (they're called partners rather than employees), a steady flow of information about the company's financial and other performance, and generous benefits. How generous? Even part-timers at Starbucks get health insurance and stock options, along with better-than-average pay at all levels.

The payoffs to the bootstrapper are twofold. First, Schultz retains experienced people—critical when you're adding a store a day. Second, he can attract new people, whom he signs on at the rate of 500 monthly. The mixture has allowed Starbucks to percolate to 1,500 outlets, 25,000 employees, and $1 billion in annual sales.

J. B. HUNT

Don't give up

Johnnie Hunt knows about being in it for the long haul. Hunt ended his education after the seventh grade to work in a sawmill. Later, his first business venture as an auction-house owner failed, leaving him deep in debt. He then struggled for years at low-paying trucking jobs to get out of hock. He quit that to begin selling rice hulls, but after a year he found himself even further in debt.

But Hunt never quit trying. He hung in while the losses turned to profits, and he eventually became one of the country's largest rice hull marketers. And when, at age 42, he started a trucking firm, he really hit high gear. Today, J. B. Hunt Transport is the country's biggest publicly held trucking company. And this school dropout is a member of the *Forbes* 400.

STEAK ESCAPE

On the surface, Bob Dille had already won. At 19, the Ashtabula, Ohio, resident snared $10,000 with a winning lottery ticket. His response? Get in the game. Not by buying more lottery tickets but by using the proceeds to purchase a Steak Escape franchise.

With two partners, Dille has played a good game since, opening new stores at the rate of one a year. Now he is co-owner of eight of the fast-food outlets and sales have topped $4.5 million a year.

You can't win if you're not in the game

CHAPTER TWO

BOOTING
UP

I started thinking about this book when I heard a public radio report about an American entrepreneur who was busy installing a string of pay phones in Somalia. His biggest expense, the announcer explained, was armed guards to protect the phones. I shook my head. Perhaps the only thing sillier would have been setting up a Pizza Hut franchise in the war zone.

There are enough obstacles to success in choosing your business. Overcoming a flawed business model shouldn't be one of them.

You need to start before you start. Figuring out which business to be in is one of the most important things you can do to ensure the success of your new venture, yet it's often one of the most poorly thought out decisions bootstrappers make.

Don't rush it. Don't just pick what you know, or what you used to do, or even what you dreamed of doing when you were a teenager. It's way more fun to run a successful vegetable stand than to be a bankrupt comedy club owner.

The first law of bootstrapping: *Great ideas are not required. In fact, a great idea can wipe you out.*

What's a great idea? Something that's never been done before. Something that takes your breath away. Something so bold, so daring, so right, that you're certain it's worth a bazillion dollars. An idea you need to keep secret.

Great ideas will kill you.

Coming up with a brilliant idea for a business is not nearly as important as finding a business model that *works*. What's a business model? This classic MBA phrase describes how you set up a business so you can get money out of it. Below are some sample business models. See if you can guess which company each comes from:

1. Hire the world's best athletes as spokespeople. Buy an enormous amount of advertising. Use the advertising to get every sporting goods store to carry your products. Make your product overseas for very little money. Charge very high prices.

2. Find local businesses that care about their employees. Offer them a free water cooler if they allow you to refill it. Earn money by making deliveries on a regular basis.

3. Create the operating system that runs every personal computer in the world. Then use the power you gain from knowing that system, which controls the computers, to create software, Web sites, online services, even travel agencies.

Right. These are the business models of Nike, Poland Spring, and Microsoft. What makes these descriptions business models? They are formulas that take the

Michael Dell found something that worked—and kept working.

In 1984, Dell began selling gray-market IBM PCs from his University of Texas dorm room. Knocking on doors at local companies, he sold all the computers he could lay his hands on. When he began buying parts and assembling his own machines, business got even better, thanks to the low prices his direct-from-manufacturer models offered to users.

After his freshman year, Dell convinced his parents to let him drop out and start selling computers full-time. He racked up $180,000 in sales his first month and never looked back. By 1998, Dell Computer's yearly revenues were $12 billion and growing.

The best proof of the value of sticking with what works came when Dell tried selling its PCs through regular retail channels. The experiment was a disaster: retailers complained about customers being cannibalized by direct deals, and customers became very confused. Dell scrapped its retail distribution scheme and returned to direct sales—still its strong point today.

A brilliant idea is not as important as a model that works

A great idea can kill you

If you attended any computer industry conferences in the late 1980s, or if you've ever seen a television special on virtual reality, you've probably seen bearded Jaron Lanier, his blond dreadlocks flying. To him, computer-created reality offered a ground-shaking, lifesaving, fortune-creating technology. As the holder of most of the key patents in the virtual reality field and founder of pioneering start-up VPL Research, Lanier was an authoritative, charismatic spokesman for what promised to be the greatest idea yet in computing.

One problem: Despite all the hype and the investments by the likes of Silicon Graphics and Disney, few uses for virtual reality were devised, fewer still were marketed, and practically none were marketed successfully. By the late 1990s, VPL Research was bankrupt. Its patents were sold to the highest bidder, while the ex-bootstrapper pursued a musical career. His great idea had nowhere to go.

assets of a company and turn them into cash. Without a business model, a company can get publicity, hire employees, and spend money—but it won't make a profit.

In a free society, the government doesn't control who gets the right to start a business. Anyone can do it—in most cases without a license, a permit, or a training course. This has one chilling implication: as soon as a business starts to make money, other people will notice, and they'll start a business just like it. This is called competition, and it usually keeps people from retiring at the age of 28.

A business model is a machine, a method, a plan for extracting money from a system. Here's another, simpler one: Buy ice cream sandwiches from a wholesaler. Put them in a refrigerated truck, drive them to the nearest beach, and sell them at retail. You make money on every ice cream sandwich you sell! (I did this in high school, by the way. I didn't make much money, but I did gain ten pounds.)

At first, this isn't such a profitable venture. But then add another layer: Buy cases and cases of ice cream sandwiches from a distributor, put them into 20 trucks, hire high school kids to sell them, and keep half the money. Suddenly, you're making hundreds of thousands of dollars a year.

Go one step further: Buy directly from the manufacturer, at an even lower price. Put your own label on the sandwiches. Then load up 200 trucks. You'll need a fleet administrator, insurance policies, and a thousand other things. But you've built a business.

At every step along the way, our fictional ice cream magnate made choices. He *chose* to bypass the supermarket. He *chose* not to advertise. He *chose* not to be the cheapest. He *chose* not to open an international branch. His path shows us all the key elements of a business model:

- *Distribution.* Where is it sold to the ultimate consumer? What middlemen are involved?

- *Sales*. Who is selling it for you and how will they be compensated?

- *Pricing*. What do wholesalers and retailers and consumers pay?

- *Production*. How do you make it?

- *Raw materials*. Where do you get what you sell?

- *Positioning*. How do the ultimate users position the product in their minds?

- *Marketing*. How do consumers find out about it?

- *Barrier to entry*. How will you survive when competitors arrive?

- *Scalability*. How do you make it bigger?

GET OFF ON THE RIGHT FOOT BY STARTING THE RIGHT BUSINESS

Understanding the mechanics of a business model is essential before you start your business. Business models should have the following five attributes:

1. *They should be profitable*. You'd be surprised at how often people start businesses that lose money on every product and then try to make it up in volume! That lemonade stand you ran when you were seven was a great lesson—you need to make money to stay in business. The only thing is that when you're seven, your mom gives you the lemons for free.

Almost no business is profitable on the very first day. The baker has to buy ovens, pay the rent, and purchase ingredients. The consultant needs business cards and brochures. The question is: How long before profitability? Write down a target date. If you go way past it, figure out how to fix the problem, or quit. Staying in a losing business because you've already lost a lot of money is a bad business strategy. Learn how to detect the factors that change a business from profitable to unprofitable. If you're contracted to deliver goods at a fixed rate but your suppliers

COLONEL SANDERS

At 66, Harland D. Sanders was ruined. A new highway routed traffic away from his Corbin, Kentucky, restaurant and forced him to close. After auctioning the physical assets, he was broke.

But he did have two assets left: his recipe for fried chicken and the plan for a new business model. That model would turn the seemingly low-value recipe into the foundation for a company whose annual sales would eventually top $8 billion.

Sanders's model was simple: he'd get restaurant owners to pay him a royalty of 4 cents for every Sanders-seasoned, "finger-lickin' good" piece of chicken they sold. The recipe of 11 herbs and spices was a hit, and his technique for using pressure cookers to reduce preparation time was another plus. But it was Colonel Sanders's pioneering model for a business franchise that built Kentucky Fried Chicken into one of the world's largest restaurant chains.

Business models turn assets into cash

DOUGLAS OTTO

They should be protect-ible

Douglas Otto's decision to license a river guide's new sandal design looked like a brilliant step for the company he'd founded, Otto's Decker Outdoor Corporation. In less than ten years, his company was selling $69 million a year worth of Teva athletic sandals.

Then trouble hit. The shoes proved easy to knock off, and cheap copies from Nike, Reebok, and others flooded the market. Worse, Otto had failed to advertise enough to give consumers a solid image of Teva as the original and quality leader. As a result of his failure to protect his niche, Teva sales dropped 31 percent in just two years and the company's debt ballooned to $10 million.

Fortunately, Otto boosted advertising, which had been just 5 percent of sales (compared with Reebok's and Nike's expenditures several times that) and began stressing Teva's quality and originality. He developed new designs to stay a step ahead of imitators. Soon, Teva sales rose and debt fell. Today, Otto's step into Teva still looks like a good one.

can raise their prices on you, you've just become a very risk-taking middleman.

There's a great cartoon of a mathematician doing a complicated proof on the blackboard. The board is covered with all sorts of squiggles and symbols and then, at the bottom, it says, "And then a miracle happens," followed by the end of the proof. Business models can't depend on miracles any more than mathematics can. Every once in a while a business comes along that creates its own model. I can tell you that it's infinitely better to have one before you start.

Using my favorite ice cream example, the business just doesn't work if implicit in the business model is the fact that you're going to lose money on every ice cream sandwich and make it up by selling more. This sort of wacked-out thinking only works on the Internet, and even there it won't work for long.

> 2. *They should be protectible*. A profitable business, as mentioned earlier, is going to attract competitors. What are you going to do when they show up? If you're accustomed to making $1 on every ice cream sandwich you sell and suddenly there's a price war, you may make only a nickel. That's not good. It's called a *barrier to entry* or *competitive insulation*. Barriers can include patents (which don't work as well as most people think), brand names, exclusive distribution deals, trade secrets (like the recipe for Coke), and something called the *first mover advantage*.

Blockbuster Video, for example, created a huge barrier to entry when it opened thousands of video stores around the country. By the time the competition showed up, all the best spots were taken. As you can guess, this is a pretty expensive barrier to erect.

First mover advantage is the fond hope that the first person into a business, the one who turns it into something that works, has an advantage over the next one. For example, if you start mowing lawns in your exclusive subdivision, the second person doesn't get a chance to solve someone's lawn problem—you've already done that. Instead, the second guy has to hope that he can undercharge or overdeliver enough to dislodge you from your spot.

3. *They should be self-priming.* One of the giant traps bootstrappers fall into is inventing business models that don't prime themselves. If you want to sell razor blades, for example, you've got to get a whole bunch of people to buy them. Without a lot of razors out there that can use your blade, you lose. Is it possible to build a paradigm-shifting business with just a little money? Sure. It's been done before. But nine times out of ten, you'll fail. Why? Because you're gonna run out of money before you change the world.

Don Katz started a business called Audible that allows you to download books on tape from the Internet. So you can find a novel you've always wanted to hear, type in your credit card number, and listen to it. The challenge Don faces, though, is that you need to buy a $150 Audible player to hear it. Without the player, it doesn't work.

So, in order to sell the books on tape (which is how he makes money), he first has to sell the player (on which he loses money). This is a business model for brave people!

Our friendly ice cream vendor has a self-priming business. Sure, he has to lay out some cash for that first truck and for the first batch of ice cream sandwiches, but after that it ought to pay for its own growth. Sell $100 worth of ice cream for $200, and you have enough money to buy yourself *two* cases of ice cream.

4. *They should be adjustable.* Remember how excited everyone got about the missiles the U.S. used during the Gulf War? Here was a weapon you could aim *after* you launched it. You could adjust the flight along the way. You need a business model like that if you're hoping to maximize your chances of success. If you've got to lock it, load it, and launch it, you're going to be doing more praying than you need to.

TOPSY TAIL

First mover advantage

Three months after Tomima Edmark's patented invention hit the marketplace in 1992, so did copycats selling at a fraction of the sales price for Topsy Tail, her new hairstyling tool. Battling the patent thieves would have cost her $250,000 and taken two years with only about a 60 percent chance of winning, she estimated.

But in reality, no court fight was necessary, because she had already won the battle of the marketplace by being there first. Edmark's three-month edge had given her the opportunity to sew up distribution channels and ink agreements with leading retailers. So although the copycats were a lot cheaper, she owned the shelf space. Edmark, a seasoned bootstrapper and the inventor of several successful products, recommends having six months to establish a successful product before competition arrives. But as her Topsy Tail experience shows, a savvy bootstrapper can succeed with even less time.

A business model that relies on a huge number of customers or partners is far less flexible than one you can adjust as you go. Subway sandwich shops, for example, have more than 13,000 locations, each individually operated. If Subway decided that the future lay in barbecued beef, it would take a lot of persuasion to get each of these entrepreneurs to go out and buy the necessary equipment. They're pretty much stuck with what they've got.

Compare this to a local restaurant with one or two locations. If everyone suddenly wants fresh oat bran muffins, they'll appear on the menu in a day or two.

The ice cream business, which you're no doubt bored with by now, is totally adjustable. In the winter you can switch to hot chocolate. If business heats up, (sorry for the pun) buy more trucks....

5. *There should be an exit strategy (optional)*. If you can build a business and then sell it, you get to extract the equity you built. If you can't sell it, all you get is the annual profit. There can be a big difference. About eight months after going public, Yahoo!, for example, had equity worth about a billion dollars, but it made only $2 in profit last year. That 500,000,000-to-1 ratio is huge, and it's unusual, and it doesn't last forever, but if your goal is a retirement villa in Cancún, the exit strategy it allows is very nice indeed.

Selling ice cream sandwiches offers no exit strategy at all until you reach a certain scale. When you're small, the business is just you. A competitor can buy trucks more cheaply than buying your business. But once you hire employees and build a brand and create trade secrets and systems, then you've built a business.

One of my favorite bootstrap businesses is the Stereo Advantage in Buffalo, New York. I was one of its first customers as a teenager in the 1970s, and since then I've seen it grow from a tiny one-room shop to a business with hundreds of employees, more than 4,000 commercial accounts, a service business, a catalog business, and a huge share of the stereo, home theater, cellular phone, and even casual clothing business in the markets in which it operates. Let's look closely at how the Advantage fares on the five rules of business models.

First of all, *it's profitable*. By relying on significant relationships with suppliers, it can buy cheap and sell sort of cheap. The profit on each sale isn't huge but the volume is, so there's plenty of money left over at the end of the day.

It's pretty protectible. In the beginning, of course, the Stereo Advantage had nothing that couldn't be easily copied. But back then, no one *wanted* to copy it. Now, twenty years later, the store has built a significant brand, a huge array of loyal customers, a talented staff, ongoing service contracts, and deep, mutually beneficial relationships with suppliers. Many, many companies have tried to go after it, but all have failed.

It's somewhat self-priming. The beginning was a very risk-filled time for the store. The owner had to buy inventory, take a lease, and hire staff without any guarantee that people like me would walk in and buy something on opening day. As it grew, though, each step has been self-priming. He brought in two televisions. When they sold, he brought in eight more. Now there are hundreds on display, without the risk that would have been incurred if he had filled the store with televisions before ever selling one.

It's adjustable. If the core of the Advantage's business is that it combines a solid reputation with a good location and trustworthy suppliers, then the business can be adjusted a great deal within those parameters. When portable telephones got hot, for instance, it was easy for Stereo Advantage's owner to talk to Sony and other suppliers and get some in the stores quickly. Same thing with home theater.

It's unlikely that the store could sell cars, or even profitably move into high-end stereos. But, within the constraints of its business model, it enjoys a great deal of flexibility.

THE DRUMMERS

There should be an exit strategy

Dyeann and Richard Dummer devoted 20 years to building *Florida Retirement Lifestyles* into the statewide voice of Florida's retirees. And they sold up to $100,000 in ads in each issue of the glossy 50,000-circulation magazine. But when the time came to get out of the magazine business, they couldn't do that profitably, and their brilliant bootstrap became something of a nightmare.

On the surface, it looked as though they had found the exit. Another, smaller publisher approached them with a buyout offer at an appealing price. He seemed to know the business and promised to improve the product by investing. Unfortunately, their buyer proved unqualified, and the terms of the sale were disastrous. Within a year, the magazine had closed its doors because the new owner had proved unable to hang on to advertisers.

The worst part? The bootstrappers had financed their buyer with a personal loan. Shortly after the magazine went under, he filed for personal bankruptcy. Now they're back in the publishing business with a plan to restart the magazine—their only hope of recouping anything from their years of effort.

PEARSON

Don't invent a business model

When Lucille Sanchez Pearson started her one-person executive search firm, she felt confident it would succeed. Why? She'd been doing the same work for her former employer, the search giant A. T. Kearney, for three years.

Not that Global Resources Ltd.—the Rolling Hills Estates, California, firm she founded in 1989—went head-to-head with Kearney. She charged clients an hourly rate instead of a percentage of the salary of the position being filled. Rather than specialize in top executives for the *Fortune* 500, she found mid-level managers for smaller firms. And instead of presenting one or two candidates, she'd research and interview as many as 100 and simply turn over the findings to a client.

The business model was similar enough to work and different enough to avoid competing directly with Kearney. That made ethical as well as business sense, figured Pearson. "I didn't want to go out and steal from the people who nurtured me in the business." In the end, ex-colleagues at Kearney wound up referring business to her, Pearson reports. And she wound up doubling her revenues every year. Within five years, her one-person business had grown to seven employees.

Which leads to the exit strategy. It's terrific. Any number of national retail chains could buy the Stereo Advantage and use it as a template for rolling out a national chain. The owner has managed to create a management team that doesn't require his personal involvement in every decision. In many ways, it's the ideal business to sell: too small to go public, but permanent enough to last beyond its founder.

Ray Kroc, one of the greatest bootstrappers ever, took a completely different tack. McDonald's (which he didn't invent, by the way) was built with the intent to "scale" it—to make it bigger.

Ray found a restaurant in California, run by two brothers. They had a system. They knew how to make a great hamburger, super fries, and a wonderful milkshake. They had a look and feel that were easy to communicate. And a way to cook.

Ray decided that growing the business was the key to competitive insulation and profits. If he was the biggest, first, he would win. So he started franchising. He let others buy the right to build their own McDonald's. The franchise deal was simple: a little money up front along with a share of the profits forever in exchange for the brand name, a rulebook, advertising, and unique products.

Let's take a look at the McDonald's business model as Ray saw it in 1965 with regard to the five principles:

It's a very profitable business. The cost of making the products is low, and a newly prosperous American public, fueled by a baby boom, is happy to pay for them.

It's very protectible. The brand name is powerful, and becomes more so every time any McDonald's on earth runs an ad. And by being first in the market, it gets the best locations, which are worth almost as much as the brand. (Did you know that in 1997, on any given day, one out of seven Americans ate a meal at McDonald's?)

It's completely self-priming. The brilliance of Ray Kroc was that he had *other people* fund his growth by paying up front for a franchise. The more he grew, the more funding he got. This is a much harder trick to pull off today, but it's not impossible.

It's not adjustable. The giant risk Kroc took was that once people bought into his franchise, they didn't want it to change. So as long as it was working for everyone, everyone was happy. But what do you do with a location that just doesn't click? How do you introduce new products when competition comes along? And what happens when you open franchises in different countries? Perhaps the biggest hassle in the franchisor's life is maintaining flexibility when there are thousands of licensees around the world.

A recent episode is a perfect example of this lack of adjustability. Burger King, seemingly stranded in second place, reformulated its way of making french fries. With a huge national campaign, it attacked one of McDonald's core products. But McDonald's couldn't possibly respond with a new recipe quickly—the logistics are too cumbersome.

The exit strategy was terrific. Ray Kroc took the company public and became a very, very rich man.

Inventing a new business model is a very scary thing. The Internet is the home of scary business models, a place where new businesses open every day, many run by people with no idea how they're going to make a living.

Yahoo!, Yoyodyne, HeadSpace, iVillage—each of these Internet marketing companies came at the marketing equation from a different angle. Each looks for a scalable, protectible model that will allow it to extract excess profits. But many Net businesses (and businesses in the real world) ignore this critical rule: *Just because it's cheap to start doesn't make it a good business.*

This is a big danger for the bootstrapper. You don't have anyone telling you you can't start a business. And if you're investing your time and just a little of your money, there's not much to stop you from giving it a try. You don't need anyone's approval!

EDDIE BAUER

Find a thriving industry and improve on the market leader

Eddie Bauer worked as a salesman, tennis racket stringer, and general roustabout at Seattle's top sporting goods store for seven years as a teenager. During that time, he learned the business inside and out. So when he opened his own tennis shop, financed by a $500 loan his father had to cosign, he was able to turn a profit from day one.

Bauer wasn't satisfied with simply replaying what he'd learned on the sales floor at Piper & Taft, however. Relying on the savvy he'd picked up on the job, he tried out ideas such as a money-back satisfaction guarantee. He specialized in stocking hard-to-get items. He constantly tried to devise new items of outdoor gear and apparel, culminating with the invention of the down-lined vest that would seal Eddie Bauer's reputation as the master source of outdoor wear.

By the time Spiegel purchased Bauer's catalog operation in 1988, the former racket stringer's company was valued at $260 million. Good use of what he'd learned working for someone else.

JUST BECAUSE IT'S CHEAP TO START DOESN'T MAKE IT A GOOD BUSINESS

Soon after Staples started opening office supply superstores, an acquaintance of mine decided that he'd start his own business. The idea was simple: He would go to larger companies and offer to sell them office supplies at a low price. He'd make the purchases at Staples and mark up the prices for his customers.

At the beginning, there was enough difference between what these organizations were used to paying for office supplies from their dealers and what Staples was charging that he could make a small profit on every sale. But my friend's idea fails most of the business model tests. The biggest problem is that once he took the time to teach these customers that price is the most important thing to look for when buying office supplies, they'd find out about Staples and switch.

This was a cheap business. He could start it for free. But it was a bad business, a business not worth the enormous investment of time and thought it takes to get started.

Don't fall into the trap of doing the easy business, or the fun business, or the sexy business. In the long run, any failed business, regardless of how cool it seems, is no fun.

The *Inc.* 500 is a list of the fastest-growing small companies in the country—and almost all of them are bootstrapped. What's interesting is how varied the businesses are, and how boring many of them are. Yet the people who are running them are having the time of their lives.

The number one company on the list makes toothbrushes. Among other companies in the top 25, there is a company that markets clip art, another that performs custodial services for corporations, and a third that markets and distributes vegetables.

DO YOU WANT TO BE A FREELANCER OR AN ENTREPRENEUR?

As you consider different business models, you need to ask yourself the critical question above. This is a moment of truth, and being honest now will save you a lot of heartache later.

The difference? A *freelancer* sells her talents. While she may have a few employees, basically she's doing a job without a boss, *not* running a business. Layout artists, writers, consultants, film editors, landscapers, architects, translators, and musicians are all freelancers. There is no exit strategy. There is no huge pot of gold. Just the pleasure and satisfaction of making your own hours and being your own boss.

An *entrepreneur* is trying to build something bigger than herself. She takes calculated risks and focuses on growth. An entrepreneur is willing to receive little pay, work long hours, and take on great risk in exchange for the freedom to make something big, something that has real market value.

If you buy a Subway franchise hoping to work just a little and get very rich, you're in for a big disappointment. The numbers of the business model don't support absentee management of most Subways. You, the franchisee, need to be the manager, too.

Contrast this with the entrepreneur who invents a new kind of photo booth, then mortgages everything he owns and borrows the rest to build a company with 60 employees in less than a year. If it works, he's hit a home run and influenced the lives of a lot of people. If it fails, he's out of the game for an inning or two and then, like all good entrepreneurs, he'll be back.

Both situations offer tremendous opportunity to the right person, and millions of people are delighted that they left their jobs to become a freelancer or an entrepreneur. But for you, only one of them will do. And you must figure out which one.

The entrepreneur is comfortable raising money, hiring and firing, renting more office space than she needs right now. The entrepreneur must dream big and persuade others to share her dream. The freelancer, on the other hand, can focus on craft. She can most easily build her business by doing great work, consistently.

This book is focused on freelancers and early-stage entrepreneurs. It's designed to show you how to thrive and survive before raising money. Because if you bootstrap successfully, you'll find that bankers, angels, and investors are far more likely to give you the money you need to grow.

The most successful bootstrappers don't invent a business model. They trade on the success of a proven one. There are countless advantages to doing this. Here are a few:

1. You can be certain that it can be done. If one or more people are making a living with this business model, odds are you can, too.

2. You can learn from their mistakes. If the guy down the street overexpands, you can learn from that.

3. You can find a mentor. Somewhere, there's someone with this same model who's probably willing to teach you what he knows.

4. You're not alone. The horrible uncertainty of staring down a bottomless pit doesn't afflict the bootstrapper who is brave enough to steal a business model.

Don't get me wrong! I'm not proposing you do nothing but copy some poor schmo, word for word, step by step. Instead, copy his business model. If there's someone making a good living selling ice cream sandwiches from a truck, maybe you could sell papayas the same way. The business model is the same—same distribution, same competitive pressures, and so on. There's plenty of room for creativity when you bootstrap, but why not take advantage of the knowledge that's there for you?

FOLLOW THE MONEY

Understanding the value chain of your business is a great first step in getting to the core of how you're going to succeed. A *value chain* is the process that a product goes through before it reaches a consumer. Starbucks, for example, starts with a coffee bean in Colombia that is so cheap it's almost free. Then they roast it and transport it and brand it and make it convenient and brew it and sell it. At each step along the way, Starbucks is adding value—making the bean worth more to its ultimate consumer. The more value you add, the more money you make.

When looking at a business model and the value chain it creates, I like to start from the last step:

1. Who's going to buy your product or service (called *product* for brevity from here on in)?

2. How much are they going to pay for it?

3. Where will they find it?

4. What's the cost of making one sale?

These four questions go to the critical issue of distribution and sales. The Pet Rock was probably the worst thing that ever happened to bootstrappers, because it led people to believe that they could turn a neat idea into nationwide distribution without too much trouble.

Nothing could be further from the truth. Getting nationwide retail distribution without money to spend on TV ads, a sales force or rep firm, and massive inventory investment is essentially impossible.

When you sell through existing retailers, *they* add a lot of the value that the consumer receives. They stock it. They make it convenient. They offer the reliability that their brand name connotes (it's guaranteed). And because they add so much value, they get to keep a lot of the profit. Look at it from their point of view. Macy's, for example, knows it's going to sell 10,000 jackets this year. They can come from Firm X or Firm Y. The Macy's purchasing agent is going to squeeze X and Y as hard as she can to extract as much profit for Macy's as she can.

If you're selling a custom service or a high-priced good, consider selling it directly. That cuts out lots of middlemen, and leaves it in your hands. If you can make this self-priming, you've gone a long way toward making your company successful.

In most products, the single largest step in the value chain is the last one—those four items in that list. If you and your company handle that last step, you've earned the right to the profit that comes with it.

For example, an architect who brings in a contractor can expect to extract more profit (or savings for his customer) than the contractor who got the job and then brought in the architect.

Obviously, some service businesses lend themselves to direct sales more than consumer products do. What if you've got your heart set on bringing a fantastic board game to market? Are you doomed to be at the mercy of mass marketers and nationwide toy chains? Not at all. There are lots of places that sell board games that aren't Toys R Us. Catalogs, for example, can help you reach large numbers of consumers without taking personal risk.

So, to recap, let's restate each of the four questions that relate to the value chain:

1. Who's going to buy your product or service?

   Define the audience.

2. How much are they going to pay for it?

   Do a value analysis to figure out what it's worth compared to alternatives.

3. Where will they find it?

Determine how much of the distribution of the product you control, and what value is added by the retailers or reps you use.

4. What's the cost of making one sale?

   Divide the cost of sales by the number of products you're going to make. You've just figured out whether they're worth selling.

The ice cream example is fascinatingly simple when it comes to these four questions.

1. Who's going to buy your product or service?

   Hot kids on the beach!

2. How much are they going to pay for it?

   Buck each!

3. Where will they find it?

   Truck comes to them—we find the best locations.

4. What's the cost of making one sale?

   It's the cost of the driver and fuel divided by the number sold over any given period of time.

This leads us to Question 5:

5. What does it cost to make, package, ship, and inventory the item you just sold?

   If you know this, you can figure out:

6. What's your profit on one sale?

   And then you can guess:

7. How many sales can you make a month?

If we add in the cost of advertising, training, overhead, and the rest, you've just mastered the value chain. And you've discovered how you can make your business profitable.

For example, let's say it costs you $5,000 a month in overhead to run the machine that makes your products. The price of each product is $2 and the cost of each is just $1. If you can figure out how to boost your sales from 5,500 units a month to 6,000 units a month (an 11 percent increase), you've just *doubled* your profits.

Business model jocks call this "sensitivity analysis." It's a way of looking at the pressure points of your business. If you know these before you even open the doors, you'll have a much better understanding of what to focus on.

Here's another example. My father makes hospital cribs. He's got a big factory filled with punch presses and painting bays and other awesome equipment. The plant is old, but it's paid for. A sensitivity analysis on his business shows that keeping the factory filled isn't the smartest thing to do. That's because labor and inventory and capital are far more expensive to him than the carrying costs on his plant. The way he can maximize his profits is by making sure that every dollar he spends on personnel turns into the maximum amount of profit. In other words, he has to either raise prices or increase productivity to make more money.

You're going to be running this business a long time. Spend an extra month to figure out what your business model feels like and save yourself some headaches later.

EVERYONE IS NOT LIKE YOU

Novelists are encouraged to "write what you know." And the business you run should reflect what you know and love and are great at.

But don't fall into the trap of assuming that everyone needs what you need, wants what you want, buys what you buy. New Yorkers run around believing that everyone has a Starbucks on every corner, while entrepreneurs in Silicon Valley are certain that everyone uses a laptop all the time.

It's so easy to extrapolate from our own experience and multiply it by 250,000,000. Don't.

When I interview people for jobs, I always ask, "How many gas stations do you think there are in the United States?" Not because I care how many gas stations there are, but because it gives me an insight into how people solve problems.

The vast majority of people who answer this question (I've asked it more than 1,000 times over the years) start their answer with, "Let's see…there are fifty states." They then go on to analyze *their* town, figure out how many gas stations there are, and multiply from there.

While this is better than some approaches, it is a ridiculous way to answer the question or to plan a business. North Dakota is not like Michigan! And your life, your neighborhood, your friends, and your needs are not like everyone else's. The best way to answer the question is to start with a scalable metric—either cars (how many cars lead to how many stations) or, surprisingly, how many big gas companies there are. Either one will get you to a quick and defensible analysis.

Instead of starting the business that makes stuff for people just like you, do some real research. Go to the library. Don't invent something that requires you to have a handle on the purchasing habits, the psychographics, and the changing demographics of the whole country. Instead, find a thriving industry and emulate and improve on the market leader. She's already done your homework for you.

Kevin Doyle loves cigars. Who wouldn't? Two years after he started Caribbean Cigar Company, his business was smoking—and how. Sales went up 1,000 percent from 1995 to 1996, Caribbean went public, and Doyle's stock was worth $20 million. But the important thing wasn't that Doyle loved cigars. The important thing was that the Miami company shipped its first smoke just as the cigar resurrection began.

But Doyle blew his stash on increasing Caribbean's capacity just as large tobacco companies started plowing cheap brands into the market. His sales shriveled, his cash disappeared, and only a multimillion-dollar loan saved him.

Now Doyle still loves cigars, but he loves marketing even more. He's investing loan proceeds to position Caribbean as a tony alternative to mass-market stogies. Building a process to support his product has taken front stage.

Your business is about the process, not the product

DON'T START A BUSINESS WHILE SHAVING! (A CAUTIONARY TALE IN SEVERAL ACTS)

As I was staring into the mirror this morning, using my brand-spanking-new Norelco razor, it occurred to me how easy it would be to start down the road to ruin while in the bathroom.

Imagine that our young hero is shaving and notices that the blades on his lift-and-cut razor aren't as sharp as they used to be. His best friend, he remembers, is a metallurgist, and maybe there would be a neat, inexpensive way to sharpen the blades in an electric razor.

A day of research in the drugstore and on the Web confirms what he already knows—there are a couple of razor-sharpening devices on the market, but they are hard to find, expensive, and not very good.

The entrepreneur arranges a business lunch with his friend. He extracts a promise to keep the big idea a secret, then describes his great insight: a low-cost razor-sharpening device that would work well.

He's got a business plan. With projections, ad slogans, a corporate mission statement, a rollout schedule, the whole thing.

"Look," he says, "there are more than five million electric razors out there. If we can sell to just ten percent of them, that's five hundred thousand units! Figure a profit of four dollars a unit and we're rolling in dough."

Following the instructions in the business books and magazines he reads, he's figured out an exit strategy and already has some angels in mind to finance the business. Right there, on a handshake, they agree to a partnership. The metallurgist will invent the device and own half the company. The entrepreneur will take it from there.

One month later, armed with plans, the entrepreneur heads for the best patent attorney he can find. He pays a $5,000 retainer and starts the process.

Then it's off to find a manufacturer. Intending to be conservative, he decides to build only 10,000 devices, noting, though, that the manufacturer needs to be able to ramp up on a moment's notice when this thing takes off like the Chicago fire.

I know what you're thinking. Wait, it gets worse.

Doing some math, our hero realizes that he needs $40,000 to pay the manufacturer. Also, he'll need to hire some sales reps to carry his item. And he figures that a TV commercial (which will run just once, because he's on a budget) will help jump-start the distribution.

Suddenly, he needs $400,000. And he's doomed.

Actually, he was doomed that first day in the bathroom.

The cost of sale is enormous. Getting the first person to buy the first sharpener is unbelievably expensive. It's a retail item, sold in a high-volume location (the drugstore). People don't know it exists and they're not sure they want it. So you have to pay a bunch of money to let people know they need one, and then you have to share a lot of the profit with the retailer.

Consumer products are almost impossible to bootstrap. Especially consumer products that need to be sold in thousands of drugstores in order to be profitable. Take a look at your local CVS—the number of bootstrapped products there is small indeed.

It gets worse.

In order to sell a product like this, it's got to be in stock when the customer gets to the store. So you'll need to make far more than you expect to sell in the next month or so, just to fill store shelves. But of course, retailers are not going to pay you in advance just to fill their shelves.

The biggest insult to the bootstrapper ethic is the fact that every customer needs only *one* for the rest of his life. That's right, after going to all the trouble of selling this item, our razor entrepreneur will never ever sell a replacement. The cost of sale is not leveraged across many sales. Hey, he won't even get the benefit of word of mouth—would you tell a friend about an invention like this?

Unfortunately, the belief that the successful entrepreneur must have in himself is a double-edged sword. Belief in a dumb business model can force you down a road that will eat away your time and your money. All the trappings of a successful business—business plan, marketing plan, finance plan, PR agency, patent lawyer, and articles of incorporation—can hide the real flaws behind a business.

And what about our hero? He gave away half the company to someone who didn't do much work and who was easily replaceable. Left with 98 percent of the work but just 50 percent of the company, he's never going to be able to raise enough money to launch this business. Lucky for him he doesn't have the cash in his retirement account—he might have been foolish enough to take the money out.

Successful bootstrappers know this: Your business is about the *process*. It's not about the product. If you structure a business model that doesn't reward you as you proceed, it doesn't matter how much you love the product. Pretty soon there won't be any product to love.

The bootstrapper is focused on finding a market that will sustain the process. A platform that responds to the work you do. With a business model that works, the deal is simple. You invest time, effort, and money. In return, your market responds with sales, cash flow, and profits.

GRAZIANO

A man and his dog. That's what it took for Philip Graziano to bootstrap his business.

Graziano was selling commercial insurance in 1996 when he and his Border collie began working part-time chasing flocks of pesky, messy Canada geese from the green corporate campuses near Flanders, New Jersey. "I kind of got into this as a joke," he recalls. Maybe it was funny at the time, but the fact that his goose-chasing gig required no up-front investment and met a need of many cash-rich prospective clients meant it had serious bootstrap potential.

"One month into it I gave up my old job," says Graziano. He wound up employing five full-time people (and nine dogs) and now boasts clients like AT&T and the real estate giant Cushman & Wakefield.

Pick a business that's friendly to boot-strappers

But, you might be thinking, don't some entrepreneurs turn big ideas into big companies? What about Steve Jobs or Bill Gates or Phil Knight or Ted Turner?

What about them? They picked giant business models and got lucky. Someone had to. The market was ready, and they won. But their success is the exception that proves the rule. For every Bill Gates there is a David Seuss, a Philippe Kahn, and 100 other super-talented, hardworking visionaries we've never heard of.

You can pick any business in the universe to bootstrap. I recommend picking one that's friendly to bootstrappers, that wants you to succeed, that will likely give back what you put in. It's easier to tell you what to avoid than to point you in the right direction. Businesses that are also hobbies usually cause bootstrappers the most trouble: restaurants, toy design and invention, creating gourmet foods.

On the other hand, mail order, consulting, acting as a sales rep or other sort of middleman, all work great. So does focusing like a laser on a very obscure market that is growing fast.

Maybe it won't make you as famous as Spike Lee or Marc Andreesen. That's okay. It will make you happy.

HOW TO BOOTSTRAP A BUSINESS THE SMART WAY

I have a friend who can do miraculous things with fabric. I've seen her turn leftover clumps of velvet into a show-stopping shawl. And she adores kids.

She decided to break into the toy business. For four years she tried to sell a better diaper bag to Fisher-Price or a new kind of catch toy to Mattel. She went to the right trade shows, got the right meetings, was careful about whom she associated with, how she positioned herself, and how she pitched her goods. She watched her expenses like a hawk. And she kept 100 percent of the equity.

There were some close calls. Fisher-Price started going to contract on the diaper bag. Mattel asked for more details. But each time, at the last minute, the company turned her down.

My friend eventually realized that she was competing in a world where she wasn't wanted. Toy companies work hard to keep inventors away, because they're scared of lawsuits and the hassles of dealing with outsiders. They're not overflowing with happy, Tom Hanks–like visionaries, looking for the next Big Idea. The toy industry is a business, and a cutthroat one.

She had made a mistake. She built a business without a business model. She tried to invent a process that could turn into a living, to become a freelancer with a royalty stream in an industry where there were very, very few role models. She could still design her clothes and bags as a hobby, but she knew it wouldn't give her enough income to make a living. She had to find another way.

She took a look around and realized that the book business publishes 50,000 new ideas every year, relies 100 percent on outsiders, and hires editors who look for ideas from the outside.

Armed with this knowledge, she spent some time getting to know her customer base. Here were 30 major publishers, all with money, all eager to buy something, all willing to pay money in advance.

Here was a totally different industry in which the process she had worked on for four years would work. The system of meeting people, inventing products, licensing them, and earning a profit—the system she had tried to build in the toy business—was working every day in the book business. Different products, same job.

After six months of hard work, she was able to get meetings with three publishers who shared her vision of the market. She listened—hard. She worked to understand what they wanted, what their customers wanted, how the industry worked.

AGENDA DYNAMICS

Plan for the money

Everybody loves a party. But if they want Janet Harris-Lange to plan their get-together, they'd better make sure it's a party with a payday.

Harris-Lange was a manufacturing executive before quitting her job to start the Lake Park, Florida, meeting-planner company Agenda Dynamics. She knew from painful experience how slow-paying or nonpaying customers could strip the profit from the best-designed product or the most perfectly planned party—unless she planned for the money. With limited resources, she knew that outlays for meeting room deposits, caterers, musicians, and employee salaries would sink her bootstrap quickly unless she could be sure the client was willing and the money was there.

So, no matter how promising the prospect, Harris-Lange takes pains to identify and avoid clients who are likely to be slow in paying their bills. Whether dealing with a government agency, a nonprofit association, or a major corporation, she checks credit reports and gathers trade references. The result? Harris-Lange's firm has four employees and a booming roster of customers. And her clients pay in an average of two weeks.

Without spending any money, My friend was able to understand the market. She was able to invent some concepts for books that she thought might sell. And then she was ready to get serious. So she found illustrators and researchers who could capture the messages she was trying to communicate. And she didn't give them equity—instead, she paid them a share of the front money.

One publisher decided that her concept for a calendar was worth a shot. They paid her a small advance and published it. Two years later, my friend's company has more than 2 million copies of her work in print. Her calendars are often at the cash register at Barnes & Noble. She's been hired as a spokesperson by a nationally marketed brand, she makes products she loves, she gets fan letters from people all over the country, and she's having fun.

Did she succeed because her calendar idea was the most unusual, original idea in the history of publishing? Or because she was a skilled novelist? Not at all. She succeeded because she understood what her market wanted and because she persevered for years and years to build her reputation. She was careful with expenses, didn't waste her equity, and set herself up for success while protecting against failure.

All without a bank loan. All without a patent lawyer. All because she picked the right business model, selling a product in a way that made sense to people who wanted to buy it.

THE SHEER JOY OF GETTING IT RIGHT

As my friend's story illustrates, when you're in the right place at the right time with the right product, you can make it work. A lot of what I'm talking about in this book might dissuade you from taking the bootstrapper journey. So many opportunities to fail, so few to succeed, it seems. But when it clicks, the magic that takes over is intoxicating. Your work, embraced by a stranger. It's a rush.

JAFFE

Changing the amount of money you need to live on can increase your success

Stephen Jaffe's bootstrap wasn't booting. The expense-reduction service the former accountant had started in his Framingham, Massachusetts, home couldn't seem to make his sales projections. Jaffe's doubtful future as an entrepreneur was placing a strain on his new wife, who was working full-time to pay their living expenses. The solution was to move from metropolitan Boston, which has one of the highest costs of living in the country, to the less costly environs of Lancaster, Pennsylvania.

The change proved refreshing in more ways than one. Once there, Stephen realized he didn't really want to be a bootstrapper. His wife, Azriela, realized she did. So he returned to work, while she wrote a book about the experience called *Honey, I Want to Start My Own Business* (Harper-Business) and began an online newsletter for couples in business. For these two, cutting living expenses opened new doors.

LEVENGER

Lori Granger and Steve Leveen started off with $8,000 and a plan to sell halogen lights by mail. But their first black-and-white catalog, making a straightforward pitch for the imported lamps' tasteful design, got a lousy response. Looking for a hook, they placed a one-inch notice in *The New Yorker* magazine advertising "Serious Lighting for Serious Readers." Orders poured in, along with requests for better reading lamps.

Their catalog, which they dubbed Levenger, began offering several lamps especially designed for readers. Soon, other reader needs such as bookends and bookcases took their place as sidelines among the general-purpose halogen lighting Granger and Leveen were still determined to focus on.

It took several months for them to read the writing on the wall. But read it they did and, letting their sideline become their main line, they rechristened the catalog with the subtitle "Tools for Serious Readers." Ten years later, the Levenger catalog carried only a few lamps among a multitude of pens, notebooks, bookstands, and other items generating annual revenues of $60 million. Not bad for a sideline.

Don't let the side-line take over (unless you want it to)

Back in 1986, when I was first starting out, I sent a direct mail letter (by Federal Express) to 40 different companies. Each firm was offered the chance to buy advertising in a book I was doing—for $1,000 a page, two pages minimum. I had figured in a huge profit margin, so all I needed was a few positive responses to make it worth the effort.

Within 48 hours, the phone started ringing. Within 30 days, I had sold more than $60,000 in advertising. It's the thrill that comes from this kind of success that keeps you going. I'm not sure that the idea behind the advertising book was the most insightful or profitable I'd ever had. But by persevering, by putting concepts in front of people in a solid, benefits-oriented way, I had succeeded.

Another time, I had the idea to create SAT prep books. The proposal went to about a dozen publishers. Most of them were a bit interested, some called for face-to-face meetings, and one or two seemed on the verge of making an offer.

We proposed to the publishers that we would auction off the right to publish these books, a common practice in the publishing world. The publisher who paid the most money at the auction would get the right to be our partner in bringing the books to market. Then an editor from Doubleday called. "Cancel the auction," she said. "What will it take to buy it right now?"

She made us an offer of about $150,000. I said it wasn't nearly enough. I was bluffing. She doubled her offer. "Nope," I said, sweating now. After two long days of her bidding and my saying no, we ended up at just over $600,000.

You'll have days like this. You'll fail and be rejected and struggle, and then you'll have days like this. Because you're a determined, focused, cheap bootstrapper intent on creating first-rate products. When those good days come, savor them!

ONE GOOD REASON NOT TO PLAN SO MUCH

Remember when I said I like to ask people how many gas stations they think there are in the United States? Well, the worst answer (and the main reason I ask) is, "I don't know."

My response is, "I know you don't know. I want you to make a smart guess."

Nine times out of ten, people refuse, in one way or another, to guess. They don't want to be wrong.

Most people hate to be wrong. They hate to make a statement (or, even worse, to write something down) and then be proved wrong. They don't like to buy the wrong car, vote for the wrong candidate, wear the wrong shoes.

Starting a business is the most public, most expensive, riskiest way of all to be wrong.

Faced with all the sensitivity analysis and business model mumbo-jumbo I talk about in this section, you might find it easy just to give up. "I'm never gonna be as smart as Bill Gates, so I give up!" Yeah, well, Bill Gates isn't so smart. Bill Gates thought the Internet was a fad. Bill Gates launched three database systems, all of which failed.

There's never been an entrepreneur with a crystal ball. There's no way to know for sure whether your business is going to work, whether your targeted customers will buy, whether your choice of technology is a good one. You're going to be wrong. Get used to it!

In the face of this uncertainty, it seems to me that the very worst thing you can do is fail to try. I went to business school at Stanford, which prides itself on being very entrepreneurial. Of the 300 people in my class, at least half publicly proclaimed that they were going to start their own businesses sooner or later.

Now, 20 years later, only about 30 of us have actually done it. The rest are still waiting for the right time or the right idea or the right backing. They're waiting for an engraved invitation and some guarantee of success.

Silicon Valley has been a tremendous boon for this country. One reason is that it has created a culture where being wrong is okay. Being wrong can even make you rich in the Valley! But in most other places, in most other families, the idea of betting your livelihood on something that might not work is a little scary.

Here's my best advice to you: Stop planning and start doing.

You don't have to quit your day job. But you do have to get out there and do it. The more you do, the more you do. Doors will open. Opportunities will appear. Your model will change, your reputation will increase, you will become a magnet for smart people, good customers, and investors. But none of this will happen if you stay inside and keep planning.

Build your business. One day at a time, one customer at a time. Lower your downsides, focus on the upsides, and start building. But start.

CHAPTER THREE

PLAN
FOR THE
MONEY

I f you don't run out of money, you get to keep playing. If you end up with more money than you started with, you win. If you *plan* for the money, and expect it, then you can avoid dwelling on it and get back to business.

Most entrepreneurs don't think about money too much when they decide to start a business. When's the last time you asked someone at a cocktail party what he does, and he responded, "Every month, I generate more cash than I spend"?

Instead, we're focused on marketing or sales or product development or hiring or firing or (God forbid) legal issues. Rarely do we deliberately plan for the money.

In some ways, this is a great policy. Money is a tool, not an end in itself for most bootstrappers. If you wanted to make big money with little risk, you'd go to Wall Street or get a fancy job for a conglomerate.

But without money, there is no business. Run out of money and your creditors will shut you down, your employees will leave, and your spouse will worry.

On at least three occasions, I've come within a few dollars of going bust. And I can tell you that it's stressful, it's distracting, and it's no fun. I also know that in each case, if I had planned for the money, it wouldn't have happened.

Planning for the money doesn't have to be complicated. But you do have to be consistent and, most of all, honest with yourself.

Start with the expense side. Make a list of every fixed expense you face month after month, no matter what. Rent. Salaries to other people. Leases. Whatever. Then add to this the *actual* average variable expenses you've faced each month over the last six months. Are you regularly spending $300 a month on travel? Put that down.

If your variable expenses vary (hey, that's no surprise!), then try to get a handle on what percentage they vary by every month. For example, if the money you spend on freelance designers over six months looks like this:

January	$1,000
February	$2,000
March	$500
April	$0
May	$2,000
June	$500

then you have an average of $1,000 a month, but a variation of as much as $1,500 a month either way.

As you build your expense analysis, create three columns:

MOST	AVERAGE	LEAST

So in this case, you'd enter

$2,000	$1,000	$0

Now, tally up your three columns. You've just figured out the *best* and the *worst* you're ever going to do in expenses.

Multiply your three numbers by 9. Now you know how much cash you need to last you nine months *if* all of your expenses are maximized *and* you have no revenue.

But of course, you *do* have revenue. It can be unpredictable. So, make two more lists. In one, list all the guaranteed revenue you've got contracts for over the next nine months. In the other one, list all the *likely* sources of revenue you expect over the next nine months.

Contracted revenue

June	$2,000
July	$18,000
August	$32,000
September	$0

Likely revenue (not counting contracted revenue)

	Minimum	Expected	Maximum
June	$4,000	$5,000	$15,000
July	$10,000	$15,000	$40,000
August	$4,000	$5,000	$15,000
September	$4,000	$5,000	$15,000

Don't kid yourself on the upside. It's one thing to be positive and optimistic in your daily life. But be a superrealist when it comes time to do revenue projections. In fact, be a pessimist. Being pleasantly surprised by an increase in revenue sure beats the alternative.

AN ACCOUNTING ASIDE

Later, when we talk about accountants, I'll go into this. But for now, let's be clear: Revenue is revenue when you *see* the money. Expenses are expenses when you *pay* the money. Cash is king and that's what you keep track of. Meaning: If you do some work but don't get paid for 90 days, you record the revenue as coming in in 90 days, not on the day that you finished the work.

Not built in to any of the numbers you've just listed is money for you to live on. That's on purpose. Once you realize that changing the amount of money you need to live on can dramatically increase your chances of success, you have an important choice to make: How much are you willing to sacrifice for the business?

One surefire way to determine if a bootstrapper is going to succeed or not is to check out how she changes her lifestyle when she starts the business. If everything is first-class—the office, the car, the mortgage, the vacations—then my bet is that the entrepreneur is too focused on taking from the business and not nearly focused enough on building it.

Jeff Bezos was a mover and shaker on Wall Street, working at the intersection of computer science and finance, when he decided to start an Internet business. Instead of maintaining his lifestyle in one of America's most expensive cities, he packed up his car and drove with his wife to a cheaper city with cheaper staffing costs where he pursued a much cheaper lifestyle. This decision was probably the most important in the success of Amazon.com. Without it, he never would have had enough money to make it to the day when investors started throwing money at him.

THE BRENTS

It started when Stephen and Julie Brents decided overseas expansion was the way to grow their small Fayetteville, Arkansas, sportswear-manufacturing company into the big leagues. They believed so strongly in the promise of foreign sourcing that when they hit a cash trough in the middle of the expansion, they started taking cash advances on personal credit cards to pay payroll and taxes. When the bills came due, they paid the minimums—often with advances from still other cards.

How long could it go on? Long enough to rack up $150,000 in plastic debt and financially destroy themselves. As sales stayed slow and interest charges mounted, the Brents said hello to Chapter 7 bankruptcy. The moral is an old one, says Stephen Brents: "We were robbing Peter to pay Paul."

If you're borrowing to pay interest, you're dead

Are you willing to move? To sell your car and buy a junker? To cut major personal expenses so you have more to invest in your business? These are critical decisions, and you need to make them with your family *before* you run out of money. Because adjusting your expense cycle then is way too late.

Here's a quick look at why saving money in advance is so much more profitable than borrowing it later.

In this chart, you can see what the bank balance of a fictional company would be under two savings scenarios. In the first, the company cuts costs so it can bank $5,000 a year at 8% interest anually for each of the first five years, then withdraws $5,000 a year in the next five years when it needs to invest in the business. In the second, it saves nothing in the first five years (meaning it spends every bit of the profits) and has to borrow $5,000 a year in each of the second five years.

SCENARIO A		SCENARIO B	
Saves	Balance	Borrows	Balance
$5,000	$5,000	0	0
$5,000	$10,400	0	0
$5,000	$16,232	0	0
$5,000	$22,531	0	0
$5,000	$29,333	0	0
($5,000)*	$26,680	$5,000	*($5,000)
($5,000)*	$23,814	$5,000	*($10,900)
($5,000)*	$20,719	$5,000	*($17,862)
($5,000)*	$17,377	$5,000	*($26,077)
($5,000)*	$13,767	$5,000	*($35,771)
			*( ) = negative

The difference is amazing. A $5,000 annual difference turns into nearly a $50,000 difference in the bottom line. That's the difference between success and failure for most businesses.

Once you've come up with your personal expense number, you have what you need to do some smart planning. You've got a nine-month look at your worst-case expenses, your guaranteed income, and your upside on both counts.

Do you have enough money in the bank to make it if *everything* goes wrong?

If you do, congratulations. Go run your business with focus and with confidence. Stick with the high road and do the things you need to realize your business plan.

If not, don't despair. You need an alternate plan. A plan that allows you to spend a percentage of your time each week on low-risk revenue sources. A way to bring in freelance income while you build your core business.

There are a lot of advantages to the multiple-income-source strategy. First, having a cash flow is a good feeling. It makes you more stable, more confident, more likely to have a successful business. Second, and just as important, those freelance gigs can easily turn into things that will help your core business.

Let's say, for example, you want to develop a career as a stand-up comic. You know it will take many months of hard work before you can expect serious income. Along the way, why not make money doing publicity for some of the clubs? Doing that can generate some money, teach you to deal with the media, and give you access to club owners. No need to charge a lot for your services— even an extra $100 or $200 a week supplementing your budget can make a big difference.

Again, the time to develop a multiple-income-source strategy is *not* when you run out of money. Then it will be too late. Right now, plan for the money.

While I'm a huge fan of the multiple-income-source strategy, there's an important caveat: Don't let the sideline take over (unless you want it to). It's so easy to get focused on the short term, on the "now," that you ignore the reason you started the business in the first place. Suddenly, it's five years later and you haven't done a stand-up gig for years. Your comedy career died the day you focused all your energy on the sideline instead of the dream.

WESTEND

Borrow money if it will generate profit

Ever heard of the basic rule of finance? Bootstrapper Roya Johnson has. So when she needed money to bootstrap her real estate brokerage off the ground, she made sure to follow it.

The basic rule of finance says you should match the terms of the source of your funds to the term of the need and the source of the repayment. Simple. If you're buying a building that's going to last a long time, you take out a 15-year mortgage. If you're buying a desk, you pay cash. For other uses, there's everything from selling investors an equity stake to taking 30-day terms from suppliers.

For Johnson, that meant she applied to the Small Business Administration for a seven-year loan of $79,000. "I figured out that if I opened that office, I could pay the loan back that quickly," she explains. And sure enough, WestEnd Properties, Inc., of Austin, Texas, generated enough profit to pay off the note, taken out in 1989, a year early.

KEEPING SCORE

Every month, you need to tally up the numbers you care about. Write them down. Share them with your spouse and board of advisers. Here they are:

Cash in this Month   ____

Cash out this Month   ____

Money in the bank right now   ____

At the current rate,
how many months
until no cash left   ____

ONE LAST THING

Debt. Debt is so seductive. You can lease computers. Use your credit cards. Mortgage your house. Borrow from relatives. Should you do it?

Let me break the debt down into two groups: professional and family.

Professional debt is expensive: 18 percent on credit cards and leases, less on a mortgage. Expensive debt carries interest that can make the problem you're trying to solve even worse. Basically, if you're borrowing money to pay the interest on borrowed money, you're dead.

My rule of thumb is that debt is bad. Available credit, on the other hand, is good. If you've got a great opportunity and *need* access to debt, you want to be able to know it's available. But living with debt regularly will enrich everyone at the banks long before it will enrich you.

Did you know that the average family in this country is carrying more than $3,000 of expensive credit card debt? This is complete lunacy. If the debt is being used to accelerate the collection of life-enhancing junk that most people buy, it's like ripping a hole in your bank account and watching the money ooze out.

Borrowing to build is the only borrowing you should do!

You should borrow money if the borrowed money is going *directly* into something that will generate profits exceeding the interest. For example, if you have a hot new device and 500 orders for it, but you can't afford to buy the parts you need to build the things, go ahead and borrow. You know you've got the sales and you'll be able to pay off the debt in 90 days. That's good use of professional debt.

On the other hand, if you're borrowing on spec, building something that you hope will sell, you've got to have the guts to stare bankruptcy right in the face. Because if you're wrong, if the opportunity disappears and the debt doesn't, you're stuck.

Even worse, if you're borrowing to pay your living expenses and salaries, trying to keep the business going just a few more months until it clicks, you're taking a similar risk. This is more pressure than yours truly can handle, but you might have a better stomach than I do.

Now, even though I've called this sort of debt "professional debt," it's almost certainly personal. Meaning that you, the boss, are *personally* on the hook for the debt. Real businesses never personally guarantee anything. When Lee Iacocca ran Chrysler, he didn't have to put up his car when the company floated a bond offering! That's why companies incorporate.

Borrowing money personally to fund your corporation is risking your personal credit. And if you're not careful, this can make it easier for other creditors to "pierce the corporate veil" and turn the actions of your company against you personally. And that's bad.

When I started, I promised myself I wouldn't personally guarantee anything, including debt. This makes it much harder to get going, but in the long run gives you a level of insulation that makes your business easier to live with. Once again, it's up to you. But once you choose a policy, stick with it.

If you personally guarantee your business, all the money you earn, from this business or any other, belongs to the bank. That means the stakes have gotten *dramatically* higher. You can't just watch this business fail and walk away. If it fails, you lose it all. And that means it will take much, much longer for you to bootstrap again.

Is your business such a sure thing that you're willing to bet everything you own on it?

Family debt is something else entirely. When I say family, I mean friends, college roommates, parents, anybody crazy enough to put up some money.

Right from the start, you've got to be clear about *why* these people are putting up money. Is it a chance for them to make some great money by investing in your business? Or is it just a vote of confidence in you, with no real expectation of repayment if you fail?

You must get all the expectations down in writing. Figure out in advance what the interest rate is, what's the term. Decide what the collateral is if you can't pay it back on time. You can really screw up some important relationships if you borrow money without both sides understanding what's at stake.

Early in my bootstrapping career, I borrowed $10,000 from my mom. As you can guess, there was no interest, and I'm not sure my mom ever expected me to pay her back quickly. But I used the money to invest in a new computer system, which led to significantly increased sales. She got her money back within six months.

Lucky for me. What if I hadn't been able to pay her back? If our expectations hadn't matched, there would certainly have been bad feelings—and we all know how quickly misunderstandings about money can damage a relationship.

Later, we'll talk about how to raise money for your business, not for you. But for now, the things to remember are:

Real businesses never personally guarantee anything

Zacky Melzer has scored a lot of victories in his battles with bankers. The founder of Tova Industries, a Louisville, Kentucky, manufacturing company, has at various times convinced bankers to lend him money at the prime interest rate—unusual for an 11-year-old company—and give him a corporate loan instead of requiring a mortgage to buy a building, saving him the cost of an appraisal and closing fees.

But Melzer's biggest victory was getting the bankers to remove his personal guarantee from Tova's loans. "That was one of my first successes," Melzer recalls. He couldn't avoid a personal guarantee at first, but after three years in business, he decided the time had come and started lobbying for the change. It took time and wasn't easy, but, as Melzer says, "Why not ask?"

1. Don't borrow money just to cover expenses.

2. Try to avoid personal borrowing at all costs.

3. When you borrow money from friends, spell out the terms.

IF YOU HAVE SALES, YOU HAVE (ALMOST) EVERYTHING

Be sales-focused. A well-financed company can afford to build a product and hope customers will come buy it. You can't. Sales before investment!

A business with plenty of sales can almost always get funding. A company with plenty of sales can almost always fix its other problems. But a company without sales is close to dead.

In chapter 2, I spent a lot of time talking about self-priming businesses. That's because a self-priming business addresses most concerns of the bootstrapper. It brings in sales before you get in too deep. It scales itself—the money you bring in can be used to garner even more money.

Sooner or later, your business comes down to extracting cash from other people or businesses and keeping as much of it as you can. It's tempting to focus on your product, your systems, your policies, the writing on page 7 of your brochure. But none of those matter if you don't have sales.

The first question to ask yourself: "Who's going to pay for this?" Whatever you create has to be so compelling that people will switch from their current solution to whatever it is that you're selling.

Please, please don't underestimate how important this is. Once you have sales, you're in the driver's seat. You can dictate whom you buy from, whom you hire, just about everything about your business.

Don't believe me? Take a look at the relationships that already exist in business. Barnes & Noble sells lots of books. That's why publishers come and beg them to carry their books. Disney gets people to wait in line to attend their movies. That's why there's a long line of actors and directors waiting to do a movie for Disney. The customer is king because the customer has money. If you figure out how to get the money, you become the king!

Here are the two most important sales rules you'll need:

1. Sell something that people want to buy (and know how to buy!). This sounds obvious, but in practice, it's not. The Edsel, for example, or jerky-flavored banana chips require a missionary sale, a level of persistence and patience that might not be worth your time. Microsoft has introduced dozens of products that have failed miserably, and so have Disney, Apple, Motorola, and lots of other well-respected (and some long-gone) companies.

Figuring out what people want to buy is a two-step process. The first step is figuring out what they're *already* buying. The second step is getting people to switch.

Let's say, for example, you've got a great idea: welcome mats for corporations— custom-made with their logo, perfect for making an even bigger impression on visitors.

Guess what? Most companies don't have someone in charge of buying this product. And if they do, that person doesn't have a budget for an item like this. And if she did, she'd hesitate because she's never bought anything like it before. What if her boss hates it? What if someone trips and sues the company? It will require bravery to buy this product, and guts and persistence for whatever salesman wants to sell it. In a nutshell, companies don't know how to buy a welcome mat, and so if you want to sell one, you've got your work cut out for you.

Do you have Post-It Notes on your desk? If so, it's only because 3M was persistent enough to spend years marketing them before they caught on. The problem was simple—they were selling something no one knew they needed. Office supplies are sold almost entirely on a reorder basis: When you run out of something, you buy more. But no one had any Post-It Notes, so they never ran out.

While a Post-It Note is a great product, the company had a serious problem. There was no one in each prospective company assigned to purchase such an item, and the cost of the sale was very, very high compared to the anticipated profit.

The solution was elegant. The chairman of 3M had his secretary send a case of Post-It Notes to the secretaries of the other *Fortune* 500 chairmen. And they started using them. Suddenly, people from the other companies were running around saying, "Hey, where can I get some of these?" And when they ran out, they had to reorder.

This was a risky bootstrap solution from a big company. If it hadn't worked, 3M would have folded the product. It's so much easier to sell something that people are already buying.

Which leads to the second question: "What will it take to get people to switch from what they already use to what I sell?"

Believe it or not, the answer is almost always *not* money. Why? Because a trusted supplier will lower her rates enough to make your offer less interesting. Why? Because switching to a low-cost supplier who does a bad job can cost the purchaser his job. Why? Because most products are purchased because of *what they do, not what they cost.*

Usually, you need to make a product that is significantly easier or more effective. Easier to buy. Easier to use. Easier to teach other people how to use. More effective at solving the problem.

Don't borrow money just to cover expenses

Muhammad Yunus started Grameen Bank in 1976 in Dacca, Bangladesh, when the university professor pulled $26 from his own pocket and lent it to a group of impoverished Bangladeshis who used it to buy materials to make chairs and pots. When the loan was repaid promptly, he made another. And another.

Today Grameen Bank has made nearly 16 million of these microloans, some as small as 65 cents, to help villagers buy cows, land, sewing machines, boats, and raw materials. All of the bank's loans are to fund business equipment and supplies; none are for consumer purchases or ongoing expenses. And despite its marginal clientele, Grameen's repayment rates top 90 percent, comparable to US credit card repayment rates.

The program is a winner for the bootstrapping borrowers, too. About half of Grameen's customers have pulled themselves and their families above the poverty line on the strength of earnings from their microfunded bootstraps. Many are repeat borrowers, funding several start-up businesses with the proceeds and employing entire families and even entire villages in their enterprises.

It didn't take long for the ballpoint pen to replace the fountain pen, did it? All you had to do was use it once to see how much more convenient it was.

It took only ten years for the word processor to completely wipe out the billion-dollar typewriter industry. Even though a word processor costs 5 to 50 times as much as a typewriter, it was much easier to use.

If a new florist opened on the corner of your block, making it much easier to buy flowers for your husband on special occasions, you'd switch in a minute. When the fax machine made it faster to send a note to someone, companies spent billions to put them in offices around the country.

Does this principle work on a local level? If you're opening a dry cleaner or becoming a freelance writer or offering accounting services, does this work for you?

You bet. A combination of more convenience, better service, aggressive pricing, and better results will make you irresistible to some people.

It won't work for everyone. Some folks may never switch. But that's okay. You don't need everyone. Just enough to keep you busy and the cash flowing!

> 2. Own the sales process.

"If a man builds a better mousetrap, the world will beat a path to his door."

No crueler words have ever been spoken. Most entrepreneurs dream about this adage being true. The fact is that it never is.

Jane Metcalfe and Louis Rossetto created *Wired*, arguably one of the best-conceived and most influential new magazines of the past 20 years. And it took them two years to get the first issue out. They spent two years, full-time, raising the money they'd need for that first groundbreaking issue.

With plenty of sales you can almost always get funding

Barbara Scallions had already spent several years as a part-time driver and, later, salesperson for a local delivery service when she decided to start her own company with $20,000 in savings. Because of her contacts and experience in sales, Congo Courier of Pflugerville, Texas, was an almost immediate success.

In fact, admits Scallions, "I was consumed by the business." A month after she started the company, four drivers were working full-time to make deliveries for customers she had landed. Her other part-time gig as a movie extra went by the wayside as Scallions concentrated on building her bootstrap. But the problems created by sales-backed growth provided their own solutions. With ample funds, she was able to invest in technology to smooth package tracking and accounting. Her solid growth qualified her for a Small Business Administration loan that enabled her to buy a building bigger than the one she was leasing, for no increase in monthly outlay.

After four years, revenues approached $500,000 a year. And Scallions was wresting with another problem: How big did she want to grow? Much expansion will require more computers, more employees, and more space. The only new sales challenge may be selling herself on the idea.

If all it took was a better mousetrap, they would have been done in about a week.

I'm not telling you this to discourage you. Far from it. If it were easy to sell, then everyone would do it and there'd be no room for your new business. No, this is a lesson you need to learn so you'll focus on the right issue.

Pick an industry—any industry. What you'll discover is that the people with power are those who either do the buying or make lots of sales. Steven Spielberg is the most powerful man in Hollywood because he can do both. Microsoft is viewed with awe because it's so good at doing both.

Follow the money! The money leads to power—the power to make decisions, the power to build the business you want to build, the power to hire and fire and shape and dream and succeed.

The pariahs who run companies that promise entrepreneurs that they will patent and protect and then license their great idea are taking advantage of people who want to delegate selling to someone else.

These companies prey on eager bootstrappers who have neat ideas and a few extra dollars. They take your dollars, do very little, and leave you broke and disillusioned.

For too many bootstrappers, sales are an afterthought. They're the thing you do that allows you to do what you really want to do. Big mistake. In fact, sales are the reason for your business to exist. If you can't sell what you make, you can't help anyone, influence anyone, or make anyone's life easier, better, or more convenient. If you can't sell what you make, you can't pay yourself. You're finished.

Here are charts showing where the monetary value is added at every step along the way for three different products:

WHEELER

"Who's going to pay for this?"

David Wheeler twice asked himself who would pay for software that analyzed crime reports. The first time, he got it wrong.

After Wheeler's father was killed in a mysterious shooting, the young database expert tackled the problem of analyzing crime scene reports, hotline tips, and other investigative information. By bootstrapping his start-up, InfoGlide, with credit cards and the sale of personal possessions, he got the funds to develop a way of reliably picking suspects from huge, messy, imprecise masses of crime data. His first market, police agencies, loved it. But they were slow-moving, budget-constrained bureaucracies. Sales were slow and sporadic. So he asked again.

This time the answer was insurance companies. They had lots of money and major problems with fraud rings that cost the industry hundreds of millions of dollars annually. In two weeks he landed deals with half a dozen top insurers for more than half a million dollars. Same product, same bootstrapper—just a different answer to "Who's going to pay for this?"

A Pair of Sneakers
(based on $80 selling price)

Materials:	$1
Assembly labor:	$3
Shipping:	$1
Price to retailer:	$40 (manufacturer keeps $35 for sales and marketing)
Price to consumer:	$80 (retailer keeps $40 for selling the shoes to you)

No doubt that the person in Scarsdale who sells the sneakers has a whopping advantage over the person in China who sews them.

Life Insurance
(share of first two years' worth of premiums, assume $400 a year)

Amount invested by company to pay your heirs when you die:	$300
Kept by company for marketing and overhead:	$100
Kept by salesperson for selling it:	$400

It's the salespeople who profit from life insurance. That's why there are so many of them!

Best-selling Book
(based on $20 selling price)

Author:	$1.70
Agent:	$.30
Printer:	$1
Price to retailer:	$12 (publisher keeps $9 for sales and marketing)
Price to consumer:	$20 (bookstore keeps $8 for selling it to you)

BOSE

Sell something people want to buy

After receiving a Ph.D. in engineering from MIT, Amar Bose decided to give himself a graduation present in the form of a new high-quality stereo system. But after looking at all the stereo speakers on the market, he was disappointed in the quality of the available models. He found that a lot of the people he talked with didn't care for then-available speakers. But nobody knew what to do about the problem. So he decided to step in.

Bose embarked on a research project to figure out what makes a good speaker. When he thought he had it figured out—part of the secret lay in aiming the speaker so listeners heard mostly reflected sound—he started a company to build and sell speakers. Bose's first 901 model came out in 1968 to rave reviews and shelf-clearing sales, and Bose went on to become one of the best-known names in audio. Thirty years later, Bose Corporation registers annual sales approaching three-quarters of a billion dollars. And all because Amar Bose knew how to listen to what people wanted.

Note that the agent who sells the book (sometimes in just a few weeks) gets 15 percent of the author's share, even though the author might have spent years writing the book. Why? Because selling is hard. And those who can sell can charge a lot for their skill.

Many bootstrappers are tempted to delegate the sales process to a representative, an agent, or an employee. Big mistake. The sales process—regardless of your business—is the heart of your business. As long as you control it, you control your company. Without it, you are at the mercy of whomever you delegate it to.

Once you have a cash flow from sales, you'll be amazed at how easy it is to buy everything else you need. As a buyer, you have all the power. You can pit suppliers against each other in bidding wars to get you the lowest price. You can find spectacular freelancers who will build, assemble, design, draw—whatever you need done, you can buy.

What should you do if you hate to sell? What if the idea of getting in front of a customer fills you with dread? Basically, you have two choices: You can find another line of work. Or you can focus all of your energy on hiring someone who can sell better than you can.

Faking your way through isn't going to work. Hoping that the sales process will go away won't help, either. As a bootstrapper you *must* sell yourself and your business. Otherwise, no business.

JON CHAIT

What will it take to get someone to switch?

Lots of people sell shoot-'em-up video games. From his experience as a Lotus Development product manager, Jon Chait knew it would take more than a lower price or a bigger ad budget to get gameplayers to switch from Doom and Duke Nukem. So before he and two partners bootstrapped a game company called Reality Byte, they developed a proprietary programming tool called RIVET that produced stunning visual graphics.

Thanks in large part to the exceptional explosions, shocking splatters, and overall out-of-this-world effects of games like Sensory Overload, Havoc, and Dark Vengeance, the three-year-old Cambridge, Massachusetts, firm has sold millions of units and grosses upward of $10 million a year. Meanwhile, Chait is improving RIVET, adding online features, and otherwise working on ways to get more twitch-and-trigger players to switch.

THE NINE MAGIC RULES OF SUCCESSFUL BOOTSTRAPPING

There are no guarantees in life, but the odds are that if you can take care of these nine things in your business, the rest will take care of itself.

RULE 1: FIND PEOPLE WHO CARE ABOUT CASH LESS THAN YOU DO

Tapping a bank for a loan when you don't yet have much to show is understandably scary. Fact is, it won't work. Banks are in business to have their loans repaid. And there are many, many businesses ahead of you in line for that money.

Sometimes it seems like the only option you have is to borrow money from friends and family.

Borrowing from other businesses to fund your business is much smarter

GEEK SQUAD

Sales are the reason for your business to exist

There are lots of computer repair companies. But there's only one Geek Squad. That fact has hurled Robert Stephens from being just another propeller-head with $200 in capital to the proprietor of a business with $500,000 annual sales in just three years.

Sure, Stephens knows his bits and bytes. And his 14 repairmen are available 24 hours a day on short notice. But what makes them special is Stephens's idea of selling his services as if he were a combination of Ross Perot and Sergeant Friday.

His servicemen show up in '50s-style black suits, driving antique emergency vehicles and brandishing badges displaying the Geek Squad logo. Stephens explains his sales approach as merely using creativity in the absence of capital. And it works.

than borrowing personal money. Your suppliers and your customers almost certainly have different objectives than you. If you can collect early and pay late, you can grow with their money.

Instead of trying to cajole a skeptical banker into lending you money on faith, borrow money from the people who have the greatest interest in your success: your suppliers and your customers.

For a minute, picture yourself as a one-person publisher who's dealing with a printing salesman under pressure to make sales. All of his old accounts are already buying the most printing they possibly can. If he makes any bonus money this year, it's going to be by creating new accounts.

That's you. A new account. Sure, you don't have much of a credit history and you're working out of your attic, but your publication just might become the next *Time* magazine.

The salesman is now on your side. He wants your business. He wants to figure out how to get the company to give you credit. After all, if you succeed, he succeeds.

Courting your big suppliers is a big part of being a successful bootstrapper. It gives you leverage. It lets you get inventory without using precious cash, saving it for those expenses you can't pay for on credit.

Best of all, when a supplier gives you extra time to pay your bills, it usually doesn't cost anything at all. That's right: zero interest.

One bootstrapper persuaded her printer to do $2 million worth of printing with no money down and 200 days to pay. In that time, she was able to build the reputation and get the advertisers she needed to make the cash flow positive. Lesson: You have to ask.

In a competitive marketplace, credit is often the tool that suppliers use to differentiate

FIRST TEAM

Find people who care less about cash than you do

John Egart just needed a push to get his in-line skate company rolling. And he thought an endorsement from Wayne Gretzky could provide it. The problem was the $500,000 that was the Great One's normal fee for endorsing products. First Team Sports, of Anoka, Minnesota, didn't have that kind of cash.

So Egart substituted creativity and spunk. He wooed and won the hockey superstar with a mix of royalties on product sales, options on First Team stock, and a special personal appeal (Gretzky's actress wife would get a role in the endorsement ad campaign) in exchange for publicly endorsing First Team's Ultra Wheels skates. Result: First Team's next-year sales nearly tripled and, by 1997, the company was the number two maker of in-line skates, doing more than $76 million in annual sales.

themselves. Take typesetting, for example. Lots and lots of folks have typesetting equipment. It's all pretty much the same. The profit margins are pretty high, but getting new customers is challenging and expensive.

My company offered a typesetter the opportunity to get $40,000 worth of new business, but he first had to agree to give us 90 days to pay his bills. My company saved tens of thousands of dollars in interest expenses, and the typesetter gained a new customer. We were both happy.

Lots of landlords will give you several months of free rent when you take space that doesn't require much interior decoration work and isn't in hot demand. Consultants, lawyers, designers—none of them have much in the way of out-of-pocket expenses, so floating you some credit doesn't cost them very much.

Another very important step in establishing credit: Be up-front with your customers and learn how to deal with them in a professional way. One thing the credit department of your target company will want is a credit history. So build one as quickly as you can. Do small amounts of business with a number of suppliers and pay cash up front. Call Dun & Bradstreet and get a report started on your company (it's free—call 800-333-0505). Tell D&B exactly whom they should quiz about your creditworthiness.

Once you've laid the groundwork, you'll be ready to start working with the essential suppliers. It helps to start with a salesperson who will take the time to teach you what you need to know.

In 1985, I cold-called Beth Emme, a printing salesperson for R. R. Donnelley, the largest printer in the world. (I figured I ought to start at the top.) I persuaded her to buy me lunch (always let the salespeople pay!) and then quizzed her for two hours. What she taught me about printing would have taken years to learn without her help.

Have a formal business reinvention process

William G. McGowan was unquestionably one of the greatest innovators in bootstrap history. Beginning with his almost unbelievably cheeky challenge to AT&T in the long distance telephone business, the cofounder of MCI Communications Corporation rolled up a list of stunning accomplishments in the field of business creativity. The Friends & Family long distance calling plans and 1-800-COLLECT discount collect calling program are just a couple of the groundbreaking ideas created by McGowan and the company he started in 1968.

How'd he do it? One of McGowan's most remarkable management tools was the requirement that all his managers trash their business plans every few months and essentially recreate their visions of the future and how they would respond to it. He explained that this kept his people from getting stale and failing to be sensitive to change in the telecommunications industry.

By the time MCI agreed to be bought by World-Com, McGowan's company was the second-largest US long-distance provider, with active businesses in everything from Internet service to cellular phones and revenues topping $30 billion. And until his death in 1992, McGowan was still requiring his people to reinvent themselves regularly.

Guess what? Over the next few years, Donnelly got lots of business from my company. They always gave me 90 days to pay my bills. I paid all their bills within a few months. And even better, Beth is now one of my best friends.

When you establish credit with your suppliers, it's important that you not go too long without paying anything. A client who makes regular payments every month is pretty hard to cut off—even if your balance is higher than they'd like.

The second great source of capital is customers. That's right. The people you're trying so hard to sell to are also a great source for money.

Remember, your product solves a problem for them. If it didn't, they wouldn't buy it. If you can't solve the problem for them, then they'll still have the problem.

My friend Sam invented a vending machine that became a huge fad. A major national chain wanted 500 machines—right away. One problem: Each machine cost $10,000 to build.

Sam frantically tried raising $5 million to pay for the machines already ordered. But the interest rates were very high, and most banks and investors didn't want to take such a big risk on a bootstrapped company.

I suggested that Sam ask the chain to pay half in advance. While it was against the chain's policy (they usually pay in 60 days, which would have been 120 days after Sam needed the money), it realized that if it *didn't* pay in advance, it wasn't going to get the machines. And the machines were worth more than money to the chain. So it paid.

Sam got his $5 million, up front, for zero interest.

Of course, sometimes it's not that easy. Sometimes you need to give the customer an incentive to pay early. A discount, or a free gift. But you won't get the money unless you ask. Always ask.

BLOCKBUSTER

Talk about a shift in perspective

What's the connection between video rental and oil-reservoir-analysis software? Answer: David P. Cook & Associates. In the mid-1980s, David Cook ran a Dallas-based software company serving the oil industry. That was when, if you recall, the bottom fell out of the energy industry. In search of a field completely unrelated to the boom-and-bust oil business, Cook started a video-rental store. He had expanded it to eight stores in the Dallas area when a wealthy Florida businessman got interested in the concept, bought Cook out, and began expanding at breakneck speed. When Viacom bought the chain for more than $8 billion, there were more than 5,000 of the stores, all carrying the original name: Blockbuster Video.

RULE 2: SURVIVAL IS SUCCESS

As you'll see in rule 5, things get better. But first, you've got to survive. If you can survive dealing with a tough project or a testy customer, do! Don't wait for the perfect pitch in the strike zone before you swing the bat.

CUC is a $2 billion publicly traded company. When it started 20 years ago, the mission was to use kiosk technology so people could buy things electronically. After raising plenty of money, CUC discovered that the technology didn't work. So it shifted the mission and started very low-tech shoppers' clubs, ones that gave CUC cash flow, plus buying power and experience.

Now, several decades later, CUC is getting into technology in a big way. It's one of the largest online stores in the world. And the business is built around those old-fashioned buying clubs. In fact, without the 20-year detour, CUC never would have learned all the valuable lessons it needed.

At the beginning, when you're armed with a plan and a cash-flow statement, you might be tempted to be very choosy about which projects and which customers you take. Don't do that! (At least not too much.) Watch the money. Take the money.

Allocate a percentage of your week to making money. Any way you can that doesn't distract from the core business. If a project makes money, it's a good project. If a product makes money, it's a good product.

The market has something in mind for you and your company. As you follow the market, as you build your reputation and your skills and your assets, new opportunities will arise.

The vast majority of start-ups go under within five years. So if you're still around, you're a winner. And it's probably because you were focused on survival.

KEITH LUCE

Associate with winners

Could working for a winner work for you? It did for Keith Luce. After years of 100-hour weeks working in some of the country's finest restaurants, Luce landed a job as sous-chef at the White House.

Luce enjoyed cooking for the Clintons and their many guests, but that was hardly the end of the tale. When his stint in the presidential kitchen ended, he parlayed his high-status connection into co-ownership of a new Chicago restaurant called Spruce. Since then, he's been named one of the country's best new chefs, and Spruce has been nominated for best new restaurant.

Don't take this survival advice too far. But take it. Money now is better than money later.

RULE 3: SUCCESS LEADS TO MORE SUCCESS

The more you do, the more you do. Being in front of people will lead to new opportunities, new products, new engagements. Be in motion, because customers like motion.

I've worked with many bootstrappers who have turned focus into a double-edged sword. They turn down work or avoid pursuing opportunities because they worry that it will keep them off the market when the right thing comes along. Sort of like the guy in high school who didn't date because he was waiting for the head cheerleader to go out with him. He didn't realize that she preferred to date someone with lots of dates.

Being busy creates its own successes. How? It:

1. Gives you positive cash flow

2. Teaches you things you didn't know

3. Builds your reputation

4. Builds your credit rating

5. Puts you in contact with smart people and potential customers

But being busy has significant downsides. The biggest one: You can really muddy your positioning. If you want to be the real estate agent who sells only expensive mansions, selling too many condos isn't going to help.

Where do you draw the line? How do you balance the desire to be busy with the focus you need to succeed?

My suggestion is that you watch your cash flow. Try to keep a reserve of six months' worth of operating expenses in the bank. When the number drops below six months, that's a message that your focus is in trouble.

Listen to your bank account!

RULE 4: REDO THE MISSION STATEMENT AND THE BUSINESS PLAN EVERY THREE MONTHS

Success brings more success, and you learn as you go. I guarantee that in six months, you'll know so much more than you do now that you'll realize your first business plan was naive.

Some bootstrappers, entranced by the legendary stories of Nike or Apple, plug along with the original vision. Hey—Bill Gates didn't set out to build the Microsoft we know today, Hewlett Packard made scientific measuring devices, and Motorola made radios.

Learn as you go. Change as you go. Building a business from scratch is like walking through a maze with many, many doors. Once you open one, 100 new doors present themselves. As you move your way through the maze, you need to stop and check your location. Look at a map. If you're in the wrong place, move. But if you've discovered a new place, there's nothing wrong with exploiting it.

You need a formal business reinvention process. Put it in your calendar. Every three months, take your most trusted advisers, employees, backers, and even customers and get away from the phones for a little while.

Start from scratch. "If we were starting over—no office, no employees, no customers— would we choose to be where we are today?" If the answer isn't yes, then it's time to take a hard look at the path you took and the impact it has had on your business.

Your path to business success is a maze, not a straight line. As the market develops, as you develop, as your employees develop, you'll discover you made some great decisions. But you also probably made some short-term decisions that became habits, and missed some opportunities because you were busy chasing something else.

Polaroid almost went under because it aggressively pursued instant movie film when it should have been chasing video. Fortunately, Polaroid realized the error in time and changed course before it was too late.

WIT Capital is an online company dedicated to raising money for other start-ups. But it used to be a brewery! The brewery did an IPO (initial public offering) online, enjoyed the process, and decided to make that the company focus. Talk about a shift in perspective.

Obviously, you have to walk a very fine line between succumbing to all the latest fads and digging in while the world changes completely around you.

That's why business-objective discussions need only happen once every 90 days or so. It makes it easy to focus on your work all the rest of the time.

RULE 5: ASSOCIATE WITH WINNERS

Four groups of people will dramatically influence how your business evolves:

1. Customers

2. Employees

3. Vendors

4. Peers

Line yourself up with the wrong people in each category and, like a poorly created bonsai tree, your business will grow up twisted and misshapen. An angry big cus-

CONNOR

Devote several hours a week to doing favors for people

Dick Connor calls his clippings the "I've-been-thinking-about-you stuff," which he sees as among the most powerful marketing tools anyone can use. As the president of his own marketing consulting firm and the author of several marketing books, Connor knows what he's talking about.

Here's how his idea works: Connor travels all the time. Anytime he gets on an airplane, he takes his address book and a handful of stamped envelopes with him. He takes the airline magazine from the seat pocket in front of him and as he scans articles, he's always asking: "Who do I know who would enjoy reading this?" And when he comes up with someone, he rips out the article, slips it into one of the envelopes, and addresses it to the client, colleague, or supplier he's got in mind. Then he drops it in the mail at his next stop.

Connor's approach is simple and easy, and it even helps him pass the time on long flights. But most important, says Connor, doing this simple favor for people is one of the most powerful ways to increase your sales, build your influence, and expand your network. In fact, says the consultant and author, "I simply can't tell you how far that goes."

tomer can force you to make concessions you'll be sorry you agreed to. Same thing with difficult vendors or pouting employees.

CUSTOMERS

Some customers are demanding, focused, responsive bellwethers for the market. After creating something for these customers, you'll discover lots of other customers wanting to buy something just like that.

Other customers are greedy and dishonest. They want you to invest in a relationship with their business and charge them the lowest price. And once the chance to switch comes along, they'll jump ship.

Other customers have horrible taste. They demand products and services that no one else could possibly want, that force you to develop skills you can't transfer, and that don't create the positive word of mouth and buzz you need.

And the last sort of customer is a jerk. He yells. He screams. He doesn't pay on time. He lies to you. He drags you into court. He bad-mouths you to others.

Want to guess which ones you need?

Most businesses wouldn't even consider firing a customer. But sometimes it's the smartest thing you can do. Several years ago, we fired one of our best customers. The company accounted for a significant percentage of our income. But its employees were nasty people. They constantly impugned my own and my employees' integrity. They threatened to violate contracts whenever they thought it would benefit them.

Tired of living in fear, we politely asked the company to find a different supplier. In the burst of energy that followed the sigh of relief we all breathed, we replaced it with four customers who generated more than twice the business.

For many companies, Microsoft is a great example of a bad customer. Microsoft frequently wants to buy products from its suppliers that the rest of the industry doesn't think are all that good. Microsoft also has a habit of learning from its suppliers and then either swallowing them up or replacing them with its own technology.

Microsoft invested (and lost) more than half a billion dollars in building its first two generations of online products (called the Microsoft Network, or MSN). The people behind MSN had an incorrect, but very confident, view of exactly what they wanted. Now, Microsoft can afford to lose half a billion dollars experimenting online. But in the process, it wiped out dozens of businesses.

Each of these bootstrappers had signed up to do Microsoft's bidding. Microsoft was so demanding that for many of them, it was their only customer. And the deals were structured so that the profits, if any, came at the back end, not up front.

When it was clear that the MSN wasn't going to make the Microsoft executives happy, they just changed direction. and wiped out whole sections of the online service in one day. And while they lived within the boundaries of their contracts, they also left their suppliers holding huge investments with no prospect of ever earning their money back—no one wanted what Microsoft had dreamed up.

Sometimes the cash you're receiving from a particular customer—even a big one—may not be worth it.

EMPLOYEES

It seems obvious that the right employee can make a huge difference to your organization. But the wrong employee can make an even bigger difference.

Are you looking for people who are smart or brave or quick or loyal or plodding or reliable or safe or attractive or obedient? Plenty of available people fit each category.

You'll discover that the time you spend managing people can have a huge impact

ERIK'S BIKE

Join a more organized peer group

Erik Saltvold opened his first bike shop at 13 and, now, at 33, has six Erik's Bike Shops in and around Minneapolis. But despite having literally grown up in the business over 20 years, Saltvold knows he doesn't know it all. When he has a question about strategy, he pedals over to Inner Circle, a peer group of other entrepreneurs he's been meeting with for five years.

None of the other members has ever run a bike shop—some haven't run anything before their current venture. But others have lots of experience in relevant areas like raising money, hiring and firing, and operating multilocation retail outlets.

No matter what issue Saltvold faces, he knows he's at least assured of a sympathetic hearing, personal support, and encouragement at their monthly get-togethers. The pats on the back—plus demands for accountability—that his peers provide are valuable spurs to his own entrepreneurial drive, especially when it comes to scary moves like adding new locations. He'd considered expanding, for instance, but had never actually done it until joining Inner Circle. Says Saltvold, "I don't think we'd have six stores now if it wasn't for my involvement in the group."

on the way you run your business. And the boldness and cleverness of your employees will directly impact the decisions you make.

If you're hell-bent on building a multimillion-dollar corporation, better be sure your employees buy into that before you hire them. And if you need an in-house skeptic to balance your proclivity to launch harebrained schemes, make sure you hire for that as well.

Employees do more than just complete the tasks you give them. They establish a pace, a culture, a tone for your company. And when they deal with the outside world, they *are* your company.

I had one employee who seemed to have a huge gray cloud of bitterness over her head. She could see the downside of every project and concluded that every deal was designed to hurt us.

She was fine at accomplishing her assigned tasks, but only after she left did I realize what a pall she had cast over my company. She had pushed the staff in a direction we didn't want to go, and I'm sorry she stayed as long as she did.

The two most important things you can do when hiring people are:

1. Make sure you have a precise, written description of both what the person is to accomplish *and* the attitudes and behaviors you want to see.

2. Hire people quickly, but hire everyone with a 60-day trial period. If a person isn't adding enough value to your company, swallow the pain and ask him to leave. If you do that, you'll feel far less pain than you would in the long run by keeping that person.

VENDORS

Can suppliers really influence your business so profoundly?

In traditional car manufacturing, each assembly point has a large supply of parts. A big bin of nuts, bolts, bumpers, whatever. If the part doesn't fit easily or is defective in some way, the line worker just throws it out and grabs the next one from the bin. This method ensures that the line never slows down.

But in making their high-quality automobiles, the Japanese use a technique called JIT (just-in-time) manufacturing. In JIT, there is only one part in the bin. The factory that makes that part is just down the street, so the part supplier makes many, many deliveries over the course of the day.

What happens if the part is no good?

The line worker hits a red button that shuts down the entire assembly line. People notice.

Guess what? The quality of parts in Japanese car factories used to be *five to ten times* better than it was here. And that led to much smarter American manufacturing and much better cars.

A simpler, smaller example is my friend Dan. Dan invented a card for the Amiga computer that used a bunch of computer chips to generate music. He bootstrapped the business from scratch and built a tremendous reputation for leading-edge components.

One reason for his success: His suppliers were quick to teach him about new parts on the market and eager to help him reengineer his products to make them faster and cheaper. A lesser supplier would have let Dan go on using more expensive, more profitable chips. But a smart supplier knew that he was better off helping Dan's business, because in the long run they'd both make more money.

The same is true for *your* business. If the vendors you work with are responsive, high-quality organizations focused on your success, you're much more likely to succeed. Obviously, not every vendor is going to meet this criterion. So you need to invest time and energy in finding alternate sources and in training and rewarding vendors to work with you better.

PEERS

These are the folks you work with or compete with or just orbit around. Even though they seem less important than the folks you buy from, sell to, or work with, they have a huge impact on how you make decisions.

Finding peers is difficult. Most bootstrappers and senior-level executives believe that they are too busy to take the time to interact when there isn't a specific business reason.

Big mistake. Networking can dramatically increase the quality of your sales efforts and your products and, best of all, increase the wisdom you gain from your work.

The best way to find peers is to devote several hours a week to doing favors for people. Favors you don't intend to have repaid. Do some favors for strangers and some for friends.

What's a favor? Sending someone a relevant newspaper clipping or e-mail message. Even better, referring business to another company that can handle it better than you. Find opportunities to brag on other companies and other people you know. You'll be meeting sometime with someone who might need to work with them.

If you interview someone who's terrific but not for you, send that person to a peer. You just made two friends! If you write an article and need a case study, ask a peer to contribute. If you deal with a business and you're happy (or unhappy) with the experience, write a letter to the president and, founder to founder, let her know how she did.

A few hours a week ought to net you a group of 100 or more peers who will benefit from your efforts as much as you'll benefit from theirs.

Another alternative is a more organized peer group. You can start one yourself or join an existing one. The Young Presidents' Organization (YPO) does this for entrepreneurs under 40 with pretty significant companies. Other groups include your local chamber of commerce or local CEO clubs.

A warning about the organized groups: Be sure to join one that's as upbeat and enabling as you are. It does you no good to sit around complaining about employees and banks and customers. You need to surround yourself with people who have succeeded and are still enjoying the ride.

I was lucky enough to be invited to address a monthly dinner club with people like that—six people who meet in Manhattan to trade war stories, play a little poker, and hear from guest speakers who can teach them something. All the group members took time to tell me how much the club had helped them build their businesses.

RULE 6: BEWARE OF SHARED OWNERSHIP (OR, WHY RINGO WAS THE LUCKIEST BEATLE)

This section might save you a fortune. It can certainly save your business. The medicine in it may seem hard to swallow, but I've been there, and so have a lot of other entrepreneurs.

In *Bargaining Games*, J. Keith Murnighan takes us through a very neat thought experiment:

Imagine receiving a phone call from a respected attorney. She tells you, "I'm sending you a ticket to France on the Concorde. Next week, on Thursday, at five p.m., you're to meet someone somewhere in Paris. You don't know who that person is. You don't know where to meet them. You can't advertise in advance to find them. He is looking for you as well. If you meet, I'll pay you twenty million dollars."

So the question is, Where would you go?

More than two-thirds of the people who answer this question give the same answer: the Eiffel Tower. It's an obvious landmark that someone searching for a noticeable meeting place might choose.

This insightful experiment shows us the way we often negotiate. In deal making, a 50/50 split is like the Eiffel Tower. It's an easy mutual agreement spot, a spot that seems fair.

Well, a 50/50 split is almost never fair. It's almost impossible to find a situation in which two people contribute equal amounts, have equal needs, have mutually consistent expectations, and will stay with the business the same amount of time.

Inevitably, someone feels cheated. And someone goes for the ride.

After Pete Best dropped out of the Beatles (okay, he was fired), John, Paul, and George needed a drummer. And Ringo was in the right place at the right time. Now, I have no idea if the Fab 4 had a four-way split, but they probably did. And Ringo, a mediocre drummer by any measure, had a great ride on the backs of three musical geniuses.

Fair? Hard to imagine that any analysis would demonstrate that Ringo deserved the same share of the Beatles as John Lennon.

Paul Allen, the cofounder of Microsoft, was probably a critical factor in that company's early success. Bill Gates certainly needed his skills during the earliest days. But today, Gates continues his monomaniacal quest for world domination, and

Advertise regularly

Rick Martis had three roommates to help pay his house mortgage and was working at a variety of sales jobs to help cover expenses, but Physical Addictions, the vitamin and workout-apparel retail store he'd cofounded, was still barely afloat. The change came when the Indiatlantic, Florida, bootstrapper noticed the classified ads that filled a fitness magazine he was leafing through and wondered whether he ought to try placing one for Physical Addictions.

He decided the answer was yes. Before long, he learned the answer should have been something like, "You'd better believe it!" Because as soon as the ad appeared, orders started flowing in. Three years later, the company passed the $1 million sales mark and today, 95 percent of its roughly $3 million in annual sales comes from mail-order ads. Martis still has the retail store, but he's now addicted to advertising, and proud of it.

Paul is lucky enough to watch his stock rise and rise in value while he doesn't even have to lift a finger.

Remember, the number one thing you have to invest is your time. And it's almost impossible to guarantee that a partner is going to invest her time in the same way or with the same impact as you. At the early stages of starting your business, it's tempting to undervalue the company, to let the experts have a big piece of the pie in exchange for getting you in the door.

One entrepreneur I know was enamored with a well-connected expert who offered to get him in the door, giving him the audience he needed with all the right clients. And the expert wanted only 20 percent of the company profits, no up-front money.

Six years later, the entrepreneur is still sweating, still working to keep the company going. And by now, the company is doing $10 million a year in sales. And that first consultant, who stopped contributing more than five years ago, still owns 20 percent of the company.

Of course, the insights and productivity that come from productive collaboration are irreplaceable.

So what should you do? Doing everything yourself is counterproductive. And being fair to the people who contribute to your business is essential. Here are five principles to consider when you sit down and start talking about shared ownership:

1. *Plan for success.* Sure, giving away stock in a failed venture costs you nothing. But imagine that your venture is going to be worth $100 million. This attitude will help you in every aspect of the business. And it especially helps focus your attention when you start taking in partners.

2. *Ideas aren't worth much.* It's so easy (and fun) to go to a bar with a

One of the most delicious ironies in all of boot-strapping is the fact that the founder of Paychex, Inc., which provides payroll-processing services to small companies, didn't receive a paycheck for the first five years he built his company. That's right. Thomas Golisano, a former accounting firm employ-ee whose idea for a payroll service was rejected by his boss, was so infused with the drive to market his idea that he paid employees with advances on his credit card and slept in his own computer room before he ever took a salary himself.

The payoff for Golisano's parsimony was rich. A decade after he started it with just $3,000 in savings, Paychex took up long-term residence on the *Inc.* magazine list of America's fastest-growing firms. After 25 years, Paychex was generating over half a billion dollars in annual sales. And Golisano processed paychecks for 250,000 clients world-wide—including, presumably, himself.

Do marketing before you take out money to pay yourself

friend or two and dream up a new business. And at the time, it seems only fair to be even partners. But usually, only one of you does all the work. And then resentment builds, and the partnership falls apart. Sometimes the whole company folds. Sometimes the arrangement is just expensive.

It's not the idea that's going to make you money. It's the sweat and the effort and the execution. If you want to brainstorm with people, that's great. But make it clear up front that the pay is the pizza on the table or a flat fee or whatever else, so long as you don't give up a piece of your company.

Here's one way to do it: "Help me dream this up. If it works, and such-and-such happens, I'll give you a check for $50,000 in cash, for your two hours [or two days or two weeks] of work. If it doesn't work, we both lose." More often than not, the party who doesn't really want to be an entrepreneur anyway will be happy to focus on the fixed number. By the way, don't forget to put your terms in writing.

When Phil Knight needed a logo for his new sneaker company, he paid a woman $35 for the design. Good for Phil that he didn't pay her with stock or just license the design!

Never give someone a big chunk of a business just because he had a great idea. There are plenty of good ideas around—free. The exception to this rule is if this person with the idea has a patent or a reputation that will dramatically expand the value of your business.

3. *Always leave both sides an out.* Nothing lasts forever, especially business partnerships. A dear friend of mine spent two years wrestling with a former partner when he left in a huff. In the end, everyone loses. Make sure you have a well-defined clause that lets either party leave without wrecking the business.

Advertising is an investment

What comes between "Double-A" and "M-C-O" ? The fact that you know the answer demonstrates the power of advertising. When Anthony A. Martino opened a transmission shop in Philadelphia in 1959, he was backed by a $3,000 loan from his father, a willingness to tackle the then-new automatic transmissions, and an unshakable faith in the power of advertising. When the first AAMCO Transmissions shop proved a success, he put the profits back into advertising. In five years, there were more than 550 franchises turning $100 million in annual sales.

Think Martino was lucky or maybe just a talented grease monkey? Probably neither, considering he later did the same thing with MAACO, an auto-body chain, the Sparks Tuneup Centers, and, recently, a child-care chain. Beep, beep.

One common approach is a shotgun clause. It says that at any point, Person A can offer to buy out Person B. Person B then has a few days either to take the money *or* to turn around and pay Person A exactly the amount proposed. It's guaranteed to be fair, and it's quick.

4. *Match compensation with performance.* An approach that's worked for a lot of bootstrappers is a performance-based split. Imagine that two partners start a business. They each own 5 percent with 90 percent in a mutually owned pool. Every six months, the 90 percent is allocated by a predetermined formula for hours invested in the business, or sales made,or products developed. Two years later, the entire 90 percent is allocated, and the partner who made the biggest contribution clearly ends up with the biggest share.

5. *Never confuse profit participation with governance.* The biggest problem with a 50/50 split is that no one is in charge. Someone *has* to be in charge. So divide control of the company differently than profit participation. Make sure that, especially in the early days, one person makes decisions. If you can't trust your partner enough to cede this to him, or vice versa, it's time to find another partner or try another business.

RULE 7: ADVERTISE

From the first day, allocate a percentage of your income to marketing. Do marketing *before* you take out money to pay yourself. Letters, phone calls, banner ads, space ads, even TV—they're all cheaper than you think. *And you've got to spend the money to get the money back.*

Here, let's repeat this paragraph, because it's that important:

From the first day, allocate a percentage of your income to marketing. Do marketing *before* you take out money to pay yourself. Letters, phone calls, banner ads, space ads, even TV—they're all cheaper than you think. *And you've got to spend the money to get the money back.*

Advertising feels like an expense. It's not. It's an investment. An investment that takes a little while to pay off, but when it does, it's magic.

The coolest thing about marketing is that when you mix two ingredients—time and money—you get an enormous return. A consistent, persistent, intelligent ad and marketing campaign, done for months or years, is nearly certain to pay off.

Remember, sales are what make your company work. And sales happen when you get access to people and they trust you. *Advertising makes sales happen.*

THE FOUR MOST IMPORTANT RULES OF ADVERTISING

I. SPEND REGULARLY ON ADVERTISING

Yes, advertising is scary. It seems like a crap shoot. You pay your money and nothing happens. You pay your money again and nothing happens. Then, after a while, it starts to pay. But most bootstrappers get impatient and give up too soon.

The way to plan your advertising is to budget for it. Figure out approximately how much your competitors advertise. (This is easy if they're buying print ads, much harder if they're using direct mail. One way to get an idea is to ask someone who doesn't directly compete with you in what they do.) Then, settle on a percentage of your revenue that will at least match, if not beat, the industry average.

Then, every month, whether you need it or not, spend that money. Spend it when times are good. Spend it when times aren't so good. Because advertising is a little like watering seeds; you don't want to miss even one cycle.

2. PERSISTENCE IS THE SECRET TO SUCCESS

In my town, a guy named Steve buys an ad every week in the local paper. Steve fixes toilets. I don't have a broken toilet right now, but you can bet that when I do, I'll dig out last week's paper and call Steve. Steve earned the sale. He bought it with a great, consistent advertisement. I trust Steve. I figure if he can afford to keep running that ad, he must be pretty good at fixing toilets.

If you persist, directing your advertising to the same people over and over and over again, you'll make a dent. Instead of always looking for a new prospect, a new audience, a new market, make sure you harvest all the apples on this tree first.

Marketers focus on two different things: reach and frequency. Reach is a measurement of *how many* different people see your ad. Frequency is a measurement of *how often* these people see your ad.

Reach is intoxicating. Buy an ad on TV and you can reach millions of people. But it's frequency that pays the bills. Here's a simple quiz to prove what I mean:

Winston tastes good…

If you knew the rest of this slogan ("like a cigarette should"), then you're like most other Americans. But this ad hasn't been broadcast in the United States since 1964! How does a slogan like this last for generations? Because of frequency. Winston burned it into our brains and our parents' brains by repeating it over and over and over again.

The secret to frequency is targeting. If you buy general advertising in a newspaper or on TV, it will be very, very expensive for you to reach the people you need, over and over. Instead, you need to use more direct media to capture the attention of your target audience.

The Stereo Advantage, which I talked about in an earlier chapter, has been running a themed ad in the same newspaper for more than 15 years. Every single Friday, the company runs a third-page ad in the *Buffalo News*, announcing their specials. You might not have seen it the first time, or noticed it the second time or read it the third time or acted on it the fourth time, but the 725th time you see the same-style ad in the newspaper, it will probably dawn on you that this store is serious and isn't about to go away!

3. BE CLEAR

You definitely don't have enough money to be obtuse. You probably don't even have enough money to be hip. What you do have, though, is an opportunity to be direct. To be blunt. To clearly and succinctly outline exactly why people should buy from you.

Have five strangers read your ad. Do they know what you do? How to contact you? What's in it for them?

Your headline is an invitation to read the rest of the ad—whether it's a letter, a billboard, or a TV commercial. If you don't get the prospects' willing participation in the ad, they'll ignore it.

Once you have them interested in the ad, you must tune in to everybody's favorite radio station: WII-FM (What's In It For Me?). Be crystal clear about what's in it for the prospects. And then make it unbelievably easy for them to do what you'd like them to do—make the contact.

4. TEST AND MEASURE

If an ad doesn't work, change one thing and try again. Measure phone calls. Measure sales. Measure inquiries.

The more you measure, the better your ad gets. Be a control freak about testing. Test one thing at a time. Make every ad you run a direct-response ad. Even if you're trying to boost your store's traffic, build in a response mechanism.

TOP OF THE TREE

Persistence is the secret of success

For Gordon Weinberger, the world ended with a phone call, not with fire or ice. He spent three years baking apple pies, using only his own ovens and fresh New Hampshire fruit, before realizing that he needed a new, more efficient facility if Top of the Tree Baking Company was ever going to turn a profit. Luckily, he'd found an investor to finance the expansion—he thought. But with a short phone call, the investor pulled out. Weinberger was out of options and, it seemed, out of business.

Devastated, Weinberger bundled his family into the car and took off for a driving vacation. But instead of running away, he was thinking. What he thought of was a new vision. He decided that if he outsourced the baking and accepted apples from outside the state, he could stay in the pie business, investor or no. And that's what he did.

Result: In a few months, Top of the Tree sales had gone from a few hundred thousand dollars a year to a few million. Weinberger had made his first foray into the profitable side of the ledger, and he'd refused to give up.

This is harder than it sounds, but it's worth it. No matter what sort of business you're running, you need to figure out a way to measure what works and what doesn't. You can insert coupons in the mailings you do. You can offer a discount if someone mentions an ad. You can (and should) have a separate phone line for the ad you run in the Yellow Pages so you can track which calls come from that very expensive ad buy.

Most of all, you should ask. No business is so impersonal that you can't talk to your customers. Take them to lunch or buy them coffee or just chat with them. Ask them what they've noticed about your marketing campaign. Ask them what finally enticed them to come visit.

Go slow. Don't be so quick to pull one campaign and replace it with an entirely different one. When you change marketing strategies, you lose all the frequency you've worked so hard to attain. And you have to start over.

As Jay Levinson, the father of guerrilla marketing, says, don't change your advertising when you get tired of it. And don't change it when your staff gets tired of it. Change it when your accountant gets tired of it.

RULE 8: GET MENTORED

Nowhere does it say you've got to do this all alone. Find someone who's come before you and ask for help. Odds are, you'll get what you ask for.

What you're doing here is pursuing the American Dream. I don't know about you, but I love seeing people succeed. And if there's a way to help someone else reach a goal, most people are eager to pitch in.

To find a mentor, you need to take some initiative. Finding the right person in the right industry at the right stage of her career takes some homework.

SYLVAN

Figure out a way to measure what works and what doesn't

If David Blohm had insisted on doing what he set out to do, he probably wouldn't have done anything. His original idea was to sell a computer program, called Sylvan's Children's Skill Test, so parents could use a quasi IQ test on their offspring at home.

Bad plan. Sales of Sylvan's Children's Skill Test were abysmal and Blohm had to do something fast to salvage the prospects of his company, Virtual Knowledge, Inc. Analyzing customer feedback, he determined what parents really wanted: a way to measure and improve their children's academic skills.

Blohm's next move was an A+. He repositioned and relaunched Sylvan's Children's Skill Test in accord with what people said they wanted. Result: The next six months' sales were nearly 200,000 units. And Blohm's once-failing company brought home $5 million worth of gold stars—all for listening to what worked and what didn't and acting on what he heard.

Lester Wunderman, the father of direct marketing and the most influential person in his industry, has been a tremendous teacher for me. So has Jay Levinson, the original guerrilla marketer, along with several other less famous but no less influential mentors I've found.

If you feel as though you're alone out there, go get some help. Not everyone will say yes (most of us are way too busy to mentor everyone we'd like to). But if you can find the right people, odds are some of them will be happy to assist you.

I recommend two steps in acquiring a mentor:

1. PICK THE RIGHT PERSON

Famous people aren't always your best bet. They're busy, they're in demand, and they may be hard to reach. And, believe it or not, they're not always the smartest people in town.

The mentor you choose should be convenient (a mentor 5,000 miles away isn't going to help you much unless e-mail is the interaction mode of choice). And he should have life experience and a network of connections that really help your business. Picking a willing mentor isn't nearly as important as picking an effective one.

2. MAKE IT EASY FOR THE MENTOR TO SAY YES AND EASY TO SAY NO

You're asking for a favor here. A big one. For that reason, you can't feel defeated if the mentor isn't interested in helping you or doesn't have the time. If that happens, overcome your natural bootstrapper desire to persist, and graciously move on.

There are lots of reasons why an individual might not want to mentor you. Time is the biggest one, of course. But there may be organizational, competitive, or personal reasons as well. You can be sure it's not about you personally, but some external factor. Let it go.

I'm a big fan of a letter, or maybe two letters, in which you lay out who you are and what you're looking for. You probably don't want to write to a stranger and say, "Hey, want to spend ten hours a week giving me free advice?" Instead, start the relationship in a simple, no-obligation way. Maybe ask the person to lunch to pick her brain. Maybe inquire about friends of friends who might be able to point you to other friends...

One woman I know is an expert networker. She has had a series of minimentors, people who help her with specific issues.

She asks her network of people, "Who do you know who's an expert on topic *x*?" Then she writes a short letter to the person who's been recommended, mentioning the person who recommended she write and asking for 15 minutes on the phone.

She calls the person's secretary, then sends the letter. Nine times out of ten, she gets her 15 minutes on the phone. She spends ten minutes exploring the issue she needs help on, then asks for (and usually gets) the names and phone numbers of three or four other people who might be able to help.

And she always sends a nice thank-you letter.

Is it hard? Not at all. Does it require preparation so she doesn't sound uninformed? Absolutely. But it is the single dynamic behind her phenomenal success—she seems to have access to any person and any information she needs.

One last thought: Never ask your mentor for more than advice. Don't ask for money. Don't ask for free output (like a designed ad or a written proposal). If you do, both of you are put on the spot. And your request will often lead to an awkward end to the relationship. Mentors don't commit for money, but for the gratification of seeing someone else succeed. They want to see *your* work pay off.

RULE 9: OBSERVE THOSE LITTLE BIRDS THAT CLEAN THE TEETH OF VERY BIG HIPPOS

My son Alex was blown away by the diorama at the Museum of Natural History in New York. There's a giant hippo, bigger than a Volvo, with its mouth open. And there, in the mouth of the beast, are a bunch of little birds.

"What are the birds doing in the hippo, Dad?" he wanted to know. As always, I told him more than he probably wanted to know. I explained that the birds eat the bugs the hippo can't get to. The birds are happy because they get an easy meal. And the hippo is happily bug-free.

There's a lot a bootstrapper can learn from these little birds. By creating a mutually beneficial relationship with a hippo, you can make a lot of money, generate credibility, and avoid being eaten.

Find bigger, richer, more stable organizations. Partner with them. It gives you credibility and access and sometimes, cash flow.

Most big-company founders hate what their companies have become. They rail against the slowness, the bureaucracy, the inability to get anything done anymore. What they need is someone like you. Someone who can take on a specific task and turn company assets into gold.

You'll be amazed at how easily you can license a brand name or do deals for ad space or take over projects for a big company. Occasionally, the company will pay you up front, just to maximize the chance of success.

Western Electric used to be the number one manufacturer of vacuum tubes (the things that glow inside old radios). Acquired by mammoth General Electric, the Western Electric factory in Kansas was defunct and the brand name was in mothballs.

An entrepreneur went to GE and licensed the Western Electric name. And he got GE to throw in the factory practically for free. GE gets some income on the margin, and the bootstrapper gets a brand heritage and a factory that would have cost him millions of dollars to build.

You'd be amazed at all the products that aren't made by the companies you *think* make them. Fisher-Price eyeglasses for kids. Sears roofing services. Flintstones vitamins. Corporations large and small are eager to find bootstrappers who can turn their wasting assets into cash.

Is it that easy? Follow nine rules and you automatically succeed? In a word, yes. But following all nine rules isn't easy. It takes commitment and concentration. You won't hit every one every day, but they're a great place to start.

CHAPTER FIVE

BEING A
PROFESSIONAL

When you come right down to it, business is in the details. And there are millions of them. Production details. Management skills. Selling approaches. Lots of tiny pieces involved in each little decision. But over time those details will add up and have a major impact on your business.

In this chapter, I'm going to describe many issues, from the way you present yourself with a business card to the powerful tools you can use to increase your sales. None of them is earth-shattering. All are important.

BUSINESS CARDS AND OTHER IMAGE MAKERS

It's a lot easier to be a bootstrapper today than it was ten years ago. Now, it's almost a badge of honor that you're working out of your house or building a business with one or two employees.

Get mentored

What's a mentor worth? One of the great family fortunes in America began with a mentor. Back in 1865 in Conover, Iowa, 21-year-old William Cargill partnered with an older businessman, H. C. Marsh, to start a business trading in lumber, hardware, and grain. Later, Cargill hooked up with a banker and investor named Jason Easton for some of his many ventures in grain warehouses, flour mills, farming, and transportation.

These mentors served Cargill well while he built a huge empire based primarily on grain storage. Eventually, he outstripped his mentors to build one of the biggest companies in the United States. Today, Cargill, Inc., still controlled by the founder's descendants, has annual sales of nearly $50 billion.

That said, remember that your prospects and your clients are judging you. You're being compared to IBM or Home Depot or some other giant company that your clients could choose instead of you.

That's why your business card should be expensive and sophisticated. And why every brochure, invoice, or sign your company creates has to be the classiest, clearest, most impressive one possible.

You're not paying for a giant corporate headquarters, TV advertising, or a battalion of Washington lobbyists. So you've got some extra money to put into the things that matter.

Spend more than you need to when it comes to making an impression. Always wear a suit to meetings, even if the guys from IBM are dressing down these days. Use a laser printer, not a dot matrix. Spell-check your documents. Type your package labels, don't scrawl them.

Trivial? Probably. But you've got to act big to get big, and when the competition has so many other advantages, it's money well spent.

RENT

One thing that most businesses have in common is that they pay rent. A lot of rent.

If you're in retail, ignore this section. Your location is everything, and generally speaking, the more you can afford to pay in rent, the better.

For the rest of us, rent is a weird expense. It's not likely to increase your profitability, and it's very easy to spend too much. You need an office for any of three reasons.

First, you need a place, as George Carlin would say, to keep your stuff. But a warehouse in the South Bronx will do just as well for this as a tony tower in Beverly Hills.

Partner with bigger, richer, more stable organiza- tions

David and Tom Gardner, on their own, didn't go from publishing an investment guide for 300 subscribers to having an America Online forum and Web site that host a combined half-million daily visitors. In fact, without a little help—make that a lot of help—the creators of the Motley Fool online investment guide would likely be languishing in obscurity instead of living on the best-seller lists (they have also written a book).

The key to their bootstrap was hooking up with America Online. They had less than $10,000 in start-up capital when they launched the Fool forum on AOL in 1994. But as AOL grew to millions of subscribers, their guide became a must-have.

Of course, it wasn't all coattails. Many online newsletters have flopped like so many PC Jrs. The brothers Gardner get credit for making their site fun, informative, and instructive. But even they admit that without AOL, the only famous Motley would still be a rock band.

KNIGHT

Kevin Knight knows he's competing with Hill & Knowlton, Edelman, and the other big names of public relations. But he never lets that stand in the way of Knight Marketing Communications, his one-person home-based company. Instead, he makes his smallness a plus.

Sure, Knight dresses in a suit and carries a leather portfolio like an account executive from the biggies. He meets clients at their places instead of in his home office and, should someone ask where he works, he just tells them that his office is "at Forest and Central," a major commercial intersection near his Dallas home.

But Knight also stresses that his service is the kind you won't get from a giant firm. With just a few clients and only one employee, he can make a strong case for any client who wants expert, personalized, intense attention. Any client who doesn't want that can look for somebody else. "If somebody wants to do business with a big company, they should do business with a big company," he says with a shrug. "You should sell yourself as special, and small."

Your prospects and clients are judging you

Second, you may need an office to attract and keep great employees (including yourself). Don't underestimate the value you get from nice, convenient, or unique office space. If you divide the incremental cost of nice space across the people you're going to have working there, it may turn out to be a cheap investment.

And third—the reason that gets many people into trouble—is that customers judge you by your location and your office. Tiffany's wouldn't be Tiffany's if it weren't on Fifth Avenue in New York. And you'd probably be unlikely to trust a heart surgeon whose office was located upstairs from a McDonald's.

If customers visit you, your office must be at least as presentable and impressive as your competitors'. Or you need to turn the difference into an asset, not something to apologize for. ABC Furniture, for example, built a huge business selling fancy furniture in a neighborhood of New York that wasn't known for furniture (or for much else, when the company started). By making an issue of the inconvenience of their location, they were able to persuade buyers that it was worth the trip—the prices and the quality more than made up for the hassle.

If customers don't ordinarily visit you, then you might be able to spend your rent money in some innovative ways. For example, you could rent a box in a nice building (even the Empire State Building offers this service) so you could have a prestigious mailing address without the cost of a full office.

You can also investigate office sharing, especially if you don't have many employees. Very few offices are actually filled. If you're friendly with someone in a bigger company, it's definitely worth pursuing an office-sharing arrangement. As a bonus, you get access to a fax machine, coffee, a water cooler, and a copier!

Before you go looking for office space, keep in mind:

- Rent is usually quoted in terms of square feet, but it's per square foot *per year.* And the square footage quoted has little or nothing to do with the actual number of square feet in the office itself. Often,

TEMPS & CO.

You need an office to attract and keep great employees

Ever apply for a job? Then you know the experience is always the same: You walk into a bland office, plop in front of a plastic desk, answer some questions, fill out some forms. Change a few details, and that's about it, right? That's what Steve Ettridge thought, too.

So the founder of a Washington, D.C., employment-agency bootstrap called Temps & Co. decided to change everything. Ettridge reasoned that the ability to attract a good supply of temporary workers was his key business skill. So he asked applicants what they did when not enduring the dehumanizing experience of applying for a job. Answers: Shop, hang out at a coffee bar, see a movie.

Next Ettridge hired a restaurant designer to come up with a new office décor. The result features indirect lighting and soft colors. Applicants relax on high chairs in front of a long bar. The feel blends bistro, coffee bar, and perfume department. The result is a 25 percent increase in walk-in applicants. Ettridge has three Job Stores, as he calls his new design for agency offices, and plans more.

overages for things like lobby space are figured in.

- The landlord will ask for a personal guarantee. Don't give one.

- A broker costs you nothing and can save you lots of time when look-ing for space.

- The landlord will offer you a "standard" lease. Nothing in this world is really standard. If you can't live with something, cross it out. One landlord offered me a lease that made us personally responsible for any fire damage to the building, even if it was caused by someone in another unit.

- Think very carefully about how long you want the lease for. Short leases seem safer, but the cost of moving and of changing addresses or phones is huge.

- If the building has multiple tenants, be sure you've got some protec-tion against them. In my company's old office, the building owner rented the room directly below us to someone who made garlic pasta for a living. The smell almost put us out of business.

- Make sure things like parking, taxes, repairs of all kinds, and pets are addressed in writing. Landlords can be nice people, but I wouldn't trust them for a minute!

- It may save you a lot of time and money to rent from a professional landlord instead of someone who's doing it as a hobby. A professional is more likely to be willing to make an investment to fix things that go wrong.

- Get references! Walk through the building and ask the other tenants what they know. Find out what they'd change in the lease if they could.

Of course, once you have an office, you'll need to find some people to fill it.

Have You Seen FAST C@MPANY?

BUSINESS REPLY MAIL

FIRST-CLASS MAIL   PERMIT NO. 137   BOULDER, CO

POSTAGE WILL BE PAID BY ADDRESSEE

FAST COMPANY

SUBSCRIPTION DEPARTMENT
PO BOX 52760
BOULDER CO 80323-2760

YOUR STAFF

Sooner or later, just about every bootstrapper is tempted to hire one or more employees. If there were only more hands, we say, we could really grow this business. There are two things to think about before you take this step—one prosaic, the other conceptual.

Once you hire someone, the government is invited to become your partner. You start paying Social Security and FICA and all sorts of taxes. You have to do withholding, and if you screw up, you're in big trouble. And you show up on every computer system in Washington.

Fortunately, a number of companies have come onto the scene eager to help you with this problem. I strongly recommend you let them handle your payroll—it's faster and cheaper in the long run. One company that specializes in small companies is Paychex.

After you've investigated the implications of this bureaucratic nightmare, you need to think long and hard about who you need and why you need them.

Your first temptation will be to hire someone just like you. After all, you work hard, you're smart, you're motivated, and you're cheap. You can make decisions, cut the right corners, and do just about everything.

Bad news. You can't hire someone just like you. Many people just like you are running their own businesses or are highly paid executives. They're not out looking to work cheap for a little bootstrapper.

No, the people you want to hire most are the people who are least like you. The organized, calm, thorough people who will follow your instructions and make your venture into a business. The caring, focused, hardworking people who don't have the vision, initiative, or risk-taking drive you do. The people who will balance your business.

Hire the people who are least like you

Richard Hayman's dad wanted somebody just like himself to take over the cash register company he bootstrapped in 1938. Richard Hayman knows better. When the elder Hayman started out, cash registers were mechanical. Today, they're computers. And who knows what lies ahead? Hayman's point: If you hire someone like yourself, no matter how successful you've been, that person is unlikely to have what it takes to handle the very different challenges that lie ahead.

Much better to hire people who can do what you can't, says the owner of 85-person Hayman Systems of Laurel, Maryland. They provide different perspectives, as well as different skills. "If you don't bring in a team of people that look at the problem from an individual viewpoint," says Hayman, "it's like building a football team with nothing but quarterbacks."

Before you try to hire someone, create a job description. Ask some friends to read it to see if it's realistic (is it really a job for four people?). Get some feeling as to whether you absolutely need to hire someone—if you can do it just as well with freelancers, that might be the way to go.

One last thought on hiring. There's a Silicon Valley expression: "A people hire A people. B people hire C people." As you build your business, you face a profound choice. You can hire the best people in their field, the A people. Or you can hire those who're just good enough.

The best people are likely to make your company the best. People who are good enough will make your company mediocre. Microsoft, one of the most successful companies of all time, invests millions of dollars a year in recruiting and screening candidates. They have tests, quizzes, personality profiles, and dozens of secret documents that make them better at picking the winners. And it works.

As a bootstrapper, without a professional human resources department, you can get yourself into a whole mess of trouble. One way you can do that is by painting an overly rosy picture of the future to your employees. Another pitfall: making promises you have no intention of keeping.

Do you really want to make your bookkeeper your partner? Are you really prepared to pay someone 10 percent of all your business, even if they stop doing a good job? Does everyone in the company really deserve a raise if the Kravitz contract comes through?

When it comes to profit sharing, raises, partnership, and other significant participation issues, *always* put things in writing. Make it crystal clear to both parties exactly what the deal entails. And be sure to leave yourself an out. Money does weird things to people, and you certainly don't want to end up in court because a sales rep decides that your entire success is due to her efforts.

The price isn't too high, the value communicated is too low

To most people, trash bags are trash bags, differentiated only by the brand name and the colors on their paper boxes. But not to customers of Ironclad, Inc. The Tustin, California, company packages its bags inside plastic containers that customers can use for kitchen storage after going through all the bags inside.

Ironclad bootstrapper John Marielli came up with the idea while considering the lack of innovation in the trash bag industry. How could he provide added utility without adding cost? The complete answer involved having two sizes of containers, making them freezer- and microwave-safe, and manufacturing them himself so the fancier packaging adds very little cost to the final product.

As a result, Ironclad's marketing costs have been flat, pricing has held the line, and yet sales have been higher. And even more important for the long run, Marielli has opened up new distribution channels since beginning the practice in 1996. That's anything but a throwaway.

People want honesty and consistency, not promises. Even if they make less money in the end, employees are far more likely to reward you with good work if they get what they expect.

Later, if things don't work out and you need to fire someone, it's going to feel terrible.

There's no magic formula here, other than telling the truth and doing it months in advance. I have no patience for the tyrannical boss who's a lousy manager and one day just screams, "You're fired."

If someone isn't doing a good job, tell him. In writing. With specific examples and specific tasks he needs to address. Sometimes he'll understand and clean up his act. Sometimes, the concept of the job is the problem, and he'll stay stuck.

But if that happens, at least the firing is depersonalized. You've outlined the behaviors needing change, and you can both agree that they didn't change. Surprise: People doing a bad job are often as happy to be gone as you are to get rid of them. It's a relief all around.

Ten years from now, when you write the history of this stage of your company, please don't blame your employees for whatever shortcomings occurred. If it's not working, you both win if they leave.

PRICING: TRICKS OF THE TRADE

Let's take a look at your house. Is it filled with used furniture from the Salvation Army? Do you drive the cheapest car available? Take the cheapest aspirin? Live in the cheapest neighborhood? You probably don't go to the cheapest doctor, eat in the cheapest restaurants, or even use the cheapest long-distance service.

If you're like most people, you don't care about getting the lowest price on everything. You care about value. About something that will solve your problem—

whatever it is—for a good price.

This is essential to remember when you think about what you're selling, whom you're selling to, and what you're going to charge for it. Many entrepreneurs make the mistake of thinking that their price is too high, when in reality, the value communicated is too low.

Several years ago, I published a book of postcards for political activists. If the book covered an issue you cared about, the postcards made it easy to make your thoughts known.

My company printed 5,000 copies of the book and priced it at $7. For a whole bunch of reasons, it didn't sell very well in the bookstores. So when the opportunity came to attend the biggest political rights rally ever held on the topic, where we could have a booth to sell the books, we jumped at the chance.

More than 500,000 people walked past our booth on that frigid April morning in Washington, DC. Probably every one of them needed and wanted the book. And probably every one of them had money on hand and was less than eight feet from the booth.

With a profit of $6 a book, we were going to make $30,000 in one day. I was already imagining clever ways to spend the money…

In the first hour, we sold one book. One.

My friend Chris, who lives in Washington, had come along to help me out. About this time, she started whining that the books weren't selling because they were too expensive. "People are here for the rally. They don't have $7 handy to spend on the book. Lower the price."

I knew, deep down, that the price had nothing at all to do with the sales problem. But I realized that someday I'd be writing a book about business and a chapter about how to price things, and this would be a great opportunity to prove my point—to Chris and to my millions of adoring readers.

So we lowered the price. To a dollar.

In the next hour, we sold two books.

The reason people weren't buying my book had nothing to do with the quality of the book. The reason was simple: At that place, at that time, this audience didn't want the benefits the book offered.

The challenge you face as you roll out your product or service is to reverse that situation. To create an environment in which the prospect needs what you have to sell and understands its benefits. Create that environment and the price is secondary.

Very important: *The cost of making something has nothing to do with what you should charge.*

Cost-based pricing works with some commodity items. But generally, it's a disaster. It will rob you of the ability to price things intelligently.

Instead, think about value-based pricing. What is your product or service *worth*? Compared to the benefits it offers and the alternatives available, what's a fair price?

If you run the only oasis in the Sahara Desert and a dehydrated man drags himself in, you can certainly charge $20 for a glass of water. He'd gladly pay double! The fact that you got the water for free is irrelevant. It's the value that matters.

You'll be amazed at how much a small increase in price can help your business. How much cash it frees up for marketing and sales expenses.

NACH-O

Test aggres- sively

Coffee bars have been followed by bagels, which have been followed by yogurt. Could there be any room left for a fourth single-item specialty food concept? And if so, would it be nachos?

You might say no, but bootstrappers Mark Gilleland, Kevin Olson, and Craig Fisher confidently said yes. Before rolling out their first Nach-O Fast shop in a Bountiful, Utah, mall food court, they surveyed mall diners and tested the concept extensively. Their conclusion: People didn't want sit-down dining, they wanted a healthy snack they could eat while shopping.

The testing paid off in sales for the first six months of more than $300,000—from a tiny unit that had cost just $15,000 to open. And when they put the concept out for franchising, it took just hours to sell 22 franchises.

Here's a simple example:

$2 cost to manufacture
$3 retail price
Your gross margin: $1
vs.
$2 cost to manufacture
$4 retail price
Your gross margin: $2

Increasing the price 33 percent in this case *doubles* your profit margin.

In most cases, the thing you sell will have no direct competition. Selling hot pretzels at the mall, for example. You're the only one. There's no direct alternative to your product. That doesn't mean you don't have competition. You do. Raise your price too much, and the benefit of the hot pretzel can be replaced by the benefit of the hot dog instead.

The best advice I can give you is to test. Test aggressively. You may discover what the president of Dreyer's ice cream did. In the early 1980s, Dreyer's was the leading creator of premium ice cream in California. In 1983, the president of the company told me that every time the Dreyer's price was raised, sales went *up*! Why? Because the higher price made it even more clear that Dreyer's was selling the *best* ice cream. In consumers' eyes, Sealtest wasn't the competition.

Dreyer's used price to define the brand—and used the extra income to buy lots of advertising and shelf space.

QUALIFY BEFORE YOU BID

Many bootstrappers make their sales through a bidding process. If you're a freelancer or a contractor, this is a fairly normal practice for you.

You have to start by recognizing that no one offers *exactly* what you do (if they do, it's time to start looking for a new line of work). Service, delivery, ease of working with you, references, guarantees, location, quality of work, reputation—all of these things contribute to the decision that the buyer will make.

So while a bidding process may seem fair and straightforward, it almost always isn't. Sometimes the bidding is to justify a decision that's already been made. Sometimes the bidding is to force the preferred bidder to lower his price.

AT&T just asked my company to bid on a major six-figure project. They wrote a fancy six-page RFP (request for proposal) that outlined exactly what they wanted. We spent weeks creating a bid and priced it very aggressively.

In the end, AT&T chose a competitor. A company that *didn't* meet all the requirements on the RFP and bid *more*. Unfair? Maybe. But shame on us for not qualifying before we bid.

To qualify a bidding process, you have to ask some questions. Here are a few starters:

- How will you be making the decision?
- Are you happy with a provider now?
- What could that provider do better?
- Who else is bidding?
- How important is *x* (service, quality, references, etc.) to you?

One of the big ways to win in this process is to set the specifications yourself. To create a need on the part of the prospect that can be met only by you.

This is not as difficult as it sounds. Even kitchen renovation, in which every contractor has access to all of the same materials and plans, is an easy place for differentiation. Selling the prospect on your guarantee, on your reputation, on how neat you will keep the worksite, or on the free set of pots and pans you throw in—whatever it is, you can make yourself unique.

OAKLEY

Guaran-tees

One of the best ways to make your company stand out is to use real, solid guarantees that you stand behind 100 percent. Big companies like Prestone antifreeze and Xerox copiers use them successfully. And giving such guarantees isn't as risky as it may sound, even for bootstrappers.

In 1989, Glen Johnson told customers of Oakley Millwork, Inc., his Frankfort, Illinois, building supplies firm, that if he ran out of any normally stocked product, they could come back and get it for free. The offer galvanized Johnson's 30 employees to make sure they never, but never, ran out of any of the 22,000 normally stocked products. As a result, in a typical year Johnson pays on only a couple of products. "The last one," he said, "cost us $42." And the payoff, on the other hand, was better than expected. Johnson attributes a 20 percent in the company's sales directly to the guarantee.

If you've done all that, price becomes secondary. In fact, price can become a weapon. You can point out that some people are cheaper, but you can't get something for nothing. Or that the other guys must be cutting corners to charge less.

A great ad runs in *AdWeek* every week. It says, "You'll pay a lot but you'll get more than you pay for."

It's often worth explaining to your clients that the value of a product is very different from its cost. Odds are, they'll forget how much they saved when the cabinets fall off and the floor is peeling. But they'll be sure to remember the great job you did every time things work the way they're supposed to.

If you've done a good job of outlining specific benefits to the prospect, you'll be in a good position to ask the big question:

If my firm meets the specs at a reasonable price, will you choose us regardless of the other bids?

This is a critical question, and it's often difficult to get an honest answer. You have to push here, but it's worth it. This is the moment that will get you or cost you the business.

If the answer is "No, the price is the key," then the next question is:

If my firm meets the specs we've described today, at the lowest price, will you choose us on the spot?

Now you're going to get the truth. Because if the answer is yes, then you've got the business if you want it. And if the answer is no, you need to explore much more aggressively what this client really wants.

SELLING TO RICH PEOPLE (OR COMPANIES) IS NO HARDER
THAN SELLING TO NOT-RICH PEOPLE

A few years ago, I took over the marketing of a summer camp in Canada. This camp had an amazing reputation and extremely loyal families, but it was losing money on every camper.

I realized that lots of families sent their kids to camp. And the main way they decided which camp was appropriate for their kids was how much it cost. Middle-class families wanted their kids to go to a middle-class camp with other middle-class kids. Rich families, on the other hand, felt that because they could pay more, they should.

In the first year, we increased the price by 35 percent. The year after that, another 20 percent. Both years, we attracted *more* campers than the year before. We did it by going after a niche. This wasn't a camp for everyone, we said. It was the *best* camp. And the message was, if you can afford it, you should come.

Obviously, there wouldn't be repeat business if we couldn't keep our promise. So we put some of that extra money into more equipment, better and fresher food, more staff, and so on. And now, eight years later, the camp is filled to capacity, with a high retention rate and a lot of happy families.

As you decide what your product is, where you're going to sell it, and what you're going to have to do to support it, think long and hard about which segment in the market you want to address.

It might be tempting to sell to entrepreneurs. But big companies will pay more. It might be tempting to sell to six-year-olds—but ten-year-olds have more money. Be opportunistic about this decision. Go where the money is.

You can make yourself unique

Vicki DeArmon started in business by dragging herself to the brink of bankruptcy. Why? By using her personal credit cards, she financed the publication of a history of the San Francisco 49ers football team. The success of the 1985 book led her to bootstrap Foghorn Press of Petaluma, California, as a sports-book publisher that by 1993 had ten employees and sales of over $1 million a year.

But then DeArmon was forced to redefine her uniqueness. A publishing-industry consolidation trend required small publishers to focus on very specialized niches, she believed. So she ditched the sports books in favor of specialty books like *California Camping* and the Dog Lover's series.

After that change, DeArmon's sales doubled in three years to $2 million. Now her goal is to extend her statewide camping and animal lovers' books to a nationwide audience and, once again, reinvent herself—this time as the nation's largest outdoor recreational guide publisher.

WHAT'S A CUSTOMER WORTH?

It seems like an odd question, but it's actually very important. Before you start spending money on marketing, you need to know exactly how much you expect to make from each customer. Not from one sale, but from your entire interaction with that customer.

Marketers call this "lifetime value of a customer." It affects two things: First, it gives you an idea of how much you ought to be investing in customer service, and second, it lets you know how much you can invest in customer acquisition.

Let's say you run a tow truck service and have the exclusive right to rescue stranded motorists on the Hamilton Skyway Bridge. For you, the lifetime value of a customer is exactly one tow. Thus, you don't care much about repeat business, and you're willing to spend a lot on each new customer.

On the other hand, American Express gets money from its customers every day, sometimes for 50 years running from a single customer. The company has determined that, on average, it's worth about $150 in direct marketing expenses to get one new cardholder. America Online, which has certainly put some floppy disks in your mailbox, is willing to spend about $105 to get a new customer.

For each of these companies, customer service for every new customer is essential. Why? Because every person who walks out the door costs them more than $100.

An ad agency might spend $20,000 or even $200,000 to get one new customer. Think they focus on retention?

LAWYERS

Some of my best friends are lawyers. My wife, in fact, is a lawyer. I just wanted to establish my credentials so you don't think I'm being too biased when you read the rest of this section.

If you let them, lawyers will suck you dry. They will become your worst enemy. They will consume your time, your energy, and your money, and they'll add almost nothing of value to your company.

This is not because lawyers are inherently evil people. They're not. At least, most of them aren't. Instead, it's because of the way they're trained, the way they're rewarded, and their desire to avoid bad things.

Here's an analogy. When you go to a doctor for a sore throat, she doesn't insist on checking you for hangnails, a bad knee, or even the heartbreak of psoriasis. Sure, she'll check to be sure there isn't some nasty tumor causing the sore throat, but generally, a doctor isn't trained to treat every patient as a potential overhaul.

Lawyers, on the other hand, quickly feel responsible for your entire company. Everything from your company handbook to your zoning, from your brochures to your contracts represents an opportunity for some other lawyer to sue you. So, to do a good job, corporate lawyers are incredibly paranoid.

Big corporations love this. They have lots of assets that folks want, so they're willing to pay millions of dollars a year to be sure that every *t* is crossed and every *i* dotted. But even the big corporations can never do enough.

That's because there are no right answers. Law is a bunch of principles, precedents, and concepts, but you can never predict what will happen in court. I can say without fear of error that if you wanted to, you could spend a $100 million in legal fees to make yourself lawsuit-proof, and even then you'd get no guarantees.

SPEND AS LITTLE TIME AND MONEY ON LAWYERS AS YOU POSSIBLY CAN

In 1981, two partners and I started a coupon-publishing business called the Boston Bar Exam. The company was going to make it easy for college students in Boston to explore new bars by publishing a book filled with coupons for free drinks.

We pooled $5,000 to get it off the ground. Then $1,000 went for logos and brochures, $1,000 went for travel and other sales expenses—and $3,000 went to our lawyers! We had fancy incorporation papers, a seal, bylaws, partnership contracts, purchase contracts, and more. At one point the two partners at the firm actually *charged* us for brainstorming about which bars might want to buy a coupon.

This was crazy. When the business failed (long story), all the fancy contracts didn't help with the dissolution. In fact, they made it harder.

The lawyers were doing what they were trained to do. They were watching our backs, expecting the worst, trying to do the right thing in advance. And we were totally stupid to follow their advice. We had nothing to lose. And we weren't going to offend anyone enough to get sued anyway.

INCORPORATE

Once you incorporate (or in some cases, become an LLC—a limited liability corporation), you've created a fictional entity that can be bought, sold, or sued. Incorporating properly (and cheaply) is a good way to spend legal money.

My favorite source for incorporation help is Corporate Agents, Inc. Their phone number is 800-877-4224. I have no idea if they're better than other such companies, but I know I've used them several times and they're a pleasure to deal with. And cheap. For $200, you're set.

Good things and bad things happen when you incorporate. The bad thing is that now the government (state and federal) knows about you. So you'll have to start filling in lots of forms.

The good thing is that with just a few exceptions, you're not personally on the hook anymore. If someone sues your company for a million bucks, fine. Fold the company and move on. Being incorporated is a great big insurance policy. The most you can lose is your business. And right now, your business isn't worth so much.

CASEY

Often, companies decide on the basis of emotion, feelings, or personalities

Quick—what color is a UPS truck? You don't even have to think before answering that one. But did you know that the ubiquitous brown vehicles might have been ubiquitous red and yellow vehicles if not for the emotional reactions of early customers of the company bootstrapped by the delivery titan James Casey?

It's true. Casey started his first delivery service with $100 in 1907 in the basement of a Seattle saloon. Six years later, the American Messenger Company bought its first delivery truck, a modified Model T the employees painted bright red. Casey painted the second truck vivid yellow, to make it stand out. It did—too well. The department stores that were his customers disliked drawing attention to the fact that they were outsourcing deliveries. To make them less visible, Casey had the trucks painted a drab brown borrowed from Pullman train cars.

And that lack of visibility paid off. UPS today has revenues of more than $20 billion and 350,000 employees, none of whom show up to deliver packages in anything but Pullman brown.

Once you build assets, once you create cash, once you reach the point where you care a lot about lawyers, then by all means, go hire a fancy lawyer.

BUY LEGAL SERVICES À LA CARTE

Never ask a lawyer what he should do for you. You might ask a lawyer what some *other* lawyer should do for you. But don't let that kid loose in your candy store!

When you have a list of what you want (see the following examples), then get some bids. Insist on a *flat fee*. Most lawyers don't like flat fees. That's exactly why you should. And don't pay for faxes, for partner conferences, for marked-up research. Instead, ask your lawyer, "How much to do this, this, and that?" And don't hesitate to have a few lawyers bid against each other (but wait until you read the next rule before you take that too seriously).

If you can't find a lawyer you like who will state a flat fee, go out and buy yourself an egg timer. A loud one with a bell. Then, whenever you call your lawyer or go to a meeting, have the timer in hand. *You* be the timekeeper.

HIRE AN EXPENSIVE LAWYER

Guess what? Expensive lawyers are almost always better than cheap lawyers. The more your lawyer charges, the better.

Of course, you want to be her lowest-paying client. You want her to take you on as a client because you have a cool business or because you're charming. Or because you offered her a seat on your board of advisers and a percentage of your profits after you make a million dollars.

Lawyers usually have horrible clients, clients who don't treat them well enough, who pay them to do boring stuff, and who have boring companies. You, on the other hand, are a breath of fresh air. The lawyer ought to pay *you* for brightening up her day.

There's an earth tremor working its way through the legal profession. The big companies aren't paying like they used to, and the explosion of small businesses hasn't made it easy for expensive lawyers to find great clients. Good for you! Be bold, be brazen. Interview audaciously.

USE YOUR LAWYER'S CONNECTIONS

Assuming you followed my advice, you now have a motivated, low-paid, expensive lawyer. You should use this for all it's worth. Have your lawyer write a letter to a big bank that handles lots of her clients, getting you access to people there. Have your lawyer introduce you to potential clients. Ask your lawyer to keep you up-to-date on new business opportunities. Of course, you shouldn't pay for any of this.

SOMETIMES YOU NEED A SPECIALIST

Your fancy, expensive (to other people) corporate lawyer is just what you need—most of the time. But if you find yourself with a copyright question or a labor law question or a challenge in dealing with the zoning board, go find a specialist. Someone who does this every day.

Because the law is vague, based on rules of thumb and inferences, the specialists almost always find a faster, cheaper, better answer. And they probably have the form you need on their word processor. And of course, bootstrappers never pay retail for a form that's already done. You might even get it for nothing if your specialist lawyer asks a friend for the form you need.

NONLAWYERS ARE GENERALLY IDIOTS WHEN IT COMES TO THE LAW

Do not take your graphic designer's advice when it comes to trademark symbols. Do not listen to your landlord when it comes to zoning. Ignore your neighbor on matters of labor law.

Go read Fred Steingold's *The Legal Guide for Starting and Running a Small Business.* Then summarize what you learned in writing and ask your lawyer if it's correct.

CASTO

"I'm the decision maker"

When Maryles Casto started her northern California travel business, she discovered in the first year where the real decision-making power lay. It wasn't with the big-company executives she was targeting as buyers of her services, despite what they said about making all the decisions in their companies.

Casto quickly learned that the real decision makers were the executive secretaries of the big bosses. They were the ones who scheduled their employers' meetings, researched travel arrangements, and booked the reservations. So Casto courted them instead of the big shots, taking them on free bus tours and otherwise softening them up for her pitch.

Casto learned that, as the bosses' attitudes suggested, the secretaries didn't get much credit for all the work they did on travel arrangements. She discovered that when she found a way to make these secretaries look like heroes—by setting up excellent plane connections, convenient hotels, and comfortable restaurants—she got so much of their business that she became a decision maker too, picking and choosing whom she'd like as clients.

WHEN TO IGNORE ALL OF THE ABOVE

There are times when the bootstrapper's approach to law is penny wise but dollar foolish. Here are two:

1. *Whenever you are about to sign a long-term contract of any kind.* A partership agreement, a lease, a multiyear supplier deal—you need a great lawyer to take his time and get it right. If you don't use one, you're likely to become an indentured servant. Your future time and opportunities are worth a fortune, so don't give them away too fast.

2. *Whenever another lawyer threatens to sue you.* If this happens, do *not* negotiate. Bring in the hammer. The killer lawyer who eats other lawyers for lunch. It will cost you money, but nine times out of ten, the other side will fold or get bought off for far less than you could have squirmed away for.

Remember: Corporate lawyers don't care about truth and justice. They care about power and winning. If your lawyer is a bully, you'll win more.

One more thing: The last bill you've got to pay is the one from your legal firm. Keep the firm happy as often as you can, but there isn't a top lawyer in America that will hassle a good customer for being a month late with a bill.

CHAPTER SIX

TOOLS
OF THE
TRADE

Sometimes, it's the odds and ends that separate the winners from the losers. As you build your business, you'll discover that you make more good decisions and few bad ones. That's no surprise—wisdom is a powerful thing, and it usually takes a long time to learn.

In this chaper, you'll discover a whole bunch of encapsulated wisdom. Ways to sell better, hire better, and keep yourself out of trouble with employees.

THE TOP TEN LIES YOU'LL HEAR WHEN YOU TRY TO SELL SOMETHING

Wouldn't it be great if you were the only person who sold what you sold? And if potential customers knew who you were and came to you just when they needed your product? Alas, reality is rarely so sweet.

People get stressed when they need to make a purchase. They worry about making a mistake, perhaps a big one, and having to live with it for years afterward. We've all been ripped off, and we've all experienced discomfort in having to say no to some salesperson.

One way people deal with this stress is by lying. They don't like to say no. They don't even like to tell the truth. Mostly because they're afraid that if you know the truth, you'll sell them something they're not prepared to buy right now.

And just about everybody you sell to has very strong feelings about the way your product should look and feel. Sometimes, customers become crazed zealots, like the folks who love the Macintosh. Other times, they turn your product into a fashion statement and make you a lot of money.

Regardless, people and companies are going to continue to set up systems and facades that make it easier for them to buy and harder for you to sell. Forewarned is forearmed.

Here, then, are ten things you'll hear over and over and how to prepare for each:

10. *"It's an open bidding situation."*

Prospects will tell you that they're looking for the best price. They're not. They almost never buy the cheapest—not the cheapest car, not the cheapest paper clip. But by describing to vendors how important the price is, they hope to get price *and* quality.

The best thinking I've ever heard on this topic comes from Zig Ziglar, author of a number of best-selling inspirational books and audiotapes. He says, "You know, years ago, our company made a decision. We decided it was better to explain the price once than to apologize for poor quality over and over and over again. And our clients are glad we made that decision."

If someone tells you that she's deciding on the basis of price, ask her to take you

SCHECHTER

Eric Schechter knows his event-marketing company does only $2 million a year, but he also knows that people know you by the company you keep. So when he pitches Great American Events Corporation to big-name clients, he offers lower prices and added features in exchange for a testimonial.

Testimonials from marquee corporations make the Scottsdale, Arizona, company seem bigger than it is, says Schechter. It helps that he knows how to use the endorsements. Customers who get the improved terms agree to be photographed, appear in advertising brochures—even receive calls from other prospects checking references.

Be ready with testimonials from similar clients

through some past bidding decisions where she made the decision that way. Was she happy about the outcome? Did the cheapest person really win? If she could do it again, what would she change?

Another great Zig comment: "Isn't it better to spend a little more than you planned and get something great than it is to spend a little less than you should have and lose everything?"

9. *"We're deciding on the basis of results.*

Most companies don't know how to measure the "results" they're talking about. Far more often, companies decide on the basis of emotion, feelings, or personalities. Anytime a prospect tells you that he's focused on results, you have a marvelous opportunity.

Inquire about which results he really measures. Ask him what's really important. And then put him on the spot: "If our product tests to be the best on x, y, and z, are you prepared to buy it today?" If the answer is yes, you win. If no, you've discovered a bluff and can get to the heart of the matter.

8. *"I'm the decision maker."*

Sometimes this is true. But more likely than not, the person you're dealing with is screening for someone else. The best way to find out is to ask the obligating question I mentioned in point 9: "Mr. Prospect, if I can show you to your satisfaction that our product does what you need, are you prepared to buy it *today?*"

The sale you're trying to make here isn't for the final sale of the product. You're selling this decision maker on recommending to his boss that his boss buy this product. If you know that you're selling to get a recommendation, it's much easier than selling for a final sale.

7. *"The budget depends on what we see."*

Asking for a budget in advance is a great way to find out whom you're dealing with and whether this is a serious opportunity. And prospects aren't going to be in

STOPKA

A sketch *isn't good* enough

How do you make a gargoyle look good? More important, why would you bother? Michael Stopka can answer both those questions, and the knowledge has been key to his bootstrapping of Design Toscano, of Arlington Heights, Illinois, a retail and mail-order statuary company.

To answer the first question, Stopka creates a dramatic, enticing atmosphere for his lushly designed catalogs by photographing statues, tapestries and other Gothic-design reproductions in fittingly exotic locales such as Notre Dame Cathedral. As a result, Design Toscano catalogs are so beautiful, he says, that customers look forward to getting them just to see what he has on the cover.

But why bother? Would growing from nothing to $12 million in sales in six years suffice?

a hurry to tell you. But they have one. They always have a budget. It's your job to find it.

You can ask questions like, "Is $x more than you planned on spending?" Or you can point to other products and ask if they're considering something like *that*.

6. *"We know all about your company and what you can do."*

You worked for years to be able to describe your company as well as you do. Don't ever skip an opportunity to describe your offerings. There's no way in the world someone walking into a meeting with you for the first time knows what you came to say. So say it.

Virtually everyone I've ever met with is willing to give me five minutes to present an overview of why I'm there and what I can do for that company. You'll get the time. Don't blow it. Instead, be ready with a focused, cogent explanation, complete with a page of testimonials from similar clients.

5. *"Just let me see it and I'll communicate it to my boss."*

See point 8. The people who get the sales are the ones who persist, who work hard to see the boss themselves.

If someone asks for materials to take to her boss, the best answer is, "I don't have anything with me today. But I've got some time, so is it okay if I wait in the lobby and you can give me five minutes with your boss sometime today?" You'll spend a lot of time in lobbies, but it may pay off.

4. *"We need it right now and we don't care about final quality."*

People always remember the quality and always forget the deadline. Name one product that succeeded because it was fast and bad. Never happens.

They'll remember the pain of the low quality long, long after they forget how hard you worked to get it done on time. "Oh, this," they never say, "it's lousy, but it was quick!"

BIRDSEYE

Clarence Birdseye didn't have enough money to finish college, and even his matrimonial plans were sidetracked by lack of funds. He had to trap furs in Canada to earn enough money to marry. That turned out to be a lucky turn of events, however, because while working in the far north, he noticed that quick-frozen fish lost little flavor when thawed and eaten. The experience stood him in good stead when, years later, he was trying to develop a method of preserving frozen foods.

Investing $7 in supplies of ice and salt and a fan, Birdseye experimented until he found a way to rapidly freeze perishables. Successful demonstrations of the process helped him line up investors to open a factory to produce frozen foods. He called the company General Foods Corporation, a name retained by the firm that purchased it several years later. Today, General Foods' Birdseye frozen-foods line thrives.

Gaining credibility early in the process is critical

3. *"A sketch is good enough."*

Clients and potential clients will always try to convince you that as trained professionals, they're not swayed by presentation. Not true. Spend the time, spend the money. If it looks good, if you look good, they'll be more confident and you'll get the sale.

This is true for engineering prototypes, Web sites, graphic designs, candy wrappers, architectural drawings, everything. It doesn't matter. If your client has ever seen a TV show, ever shopped in a supermarket, ever surfed the Web, you can bet his expectations are set at a certain level.

2. *"I don't want to be a backseat driver, but…"*

Every American believes he has two inalienable rights: to be president of the United States and to direct a major Hollywood motion picture. Beware the backseat driver.

After you make the sale conceptually, you need to sell the client on leaving you alone to do great work. Get your agreement in writing. Build in milestones. Make it clear to both sides that the client's input is vital but that he's hiring you because you're great at what you do.

And the number-one lie:

1. *"I'll know it when I see it."*

Well, yes and no. There are many, many people who can't put into words what it is that they want to buy. They basically troll around looking for something that magically touches them. So that's true. But sometimes, in their zest to see everything, they fail to mention their own requirements—the features you must know about to make your product a success.

I recently went through a month of trying to hire someone. (I think of hiring itself as a particular kind of sale.) This candidate explained in great detail that she'd know the right job when she saw it. We gave her references, had her spend time with enthusiastic employees, and focused a lot of time and energy on her.

In the end, she took a different job. Why? Because it was located in Manhattan, so she wouldn't have to commute. I'd asked her about that in the *first* interview. She never told me what she wanted, so I couldn't save us both time.

Great salespeople are good at getting prospects to tell the truth.

THE TOP TEN PRINCIPLES THAT MAKE IT EASIER TO WORK WITH CLIENTS

Unless you sell can openers or tuna fish, it's likely you're going to have to work with clients before, during, and after the sale. In order to build a satisfied customer base and generate positive word of mouth, you're going to have to focus on the customer satisfaction process.

Here are ten things that make it easier to work with a potential or existing client over time:

10. *Realize you are selling.*

Be formal and overt. Better to err on the side of making a big deal of the selling process than to slink into it. If a prospect says, "Hey, are you trying to sell me something?" better be ready with a quick and enthusiastic "Yes!"

If you believe you're solving a problem, supplying a great product for less money, then you don't just have the right to sell. You have an obligation to sell. Don't walk out of the meeting without giving your full effort.

9. *Ask lots of questions.*

Make sure the client has a chance to tell you what she likes, what she doesn't like, what the real deadlines are, who can approve what, how likely they are to want to noodle with stuff, what an example of a *great* product was in the past, and what four words she'd like to use to describe the finished product or service she's actually going to buy.

Nine times out of ten, if you miss a sale it will be because you talked too much and didn't ask enough questions.

8. *If you are selling custom products or services, build in sufficient review cycles so that you never have to tell the client that the choice is between making a change or busting the schedule.*

The customer is always right. Because if you tell them that they're wrong, then they can choose not to be your customer anymore. Whether you are a caterer, a gardener, a grocer, or a lawyer, clearly outlining the review cycles will always pay off.

7. *At the same time, build in milestones solid enough that the client understands the implications of not sticking to the agreed terms.*

Customers are usually rational. They'll happily stick to the rules if they understand what the rules are. For example, if a reception hall you've booked for a customer's wedding charges a 25 percent cancellation fee for backing out, and the fee is clearly stated in the contract, then the customer will accept having to pay the fee.

6. *Work very hard to establish your credentials, so your client is likely to believe what you say.*

Gaining credibility early in the process is critical. It will give you the leverage you need to do your job properly when inevitable disagreements occur. Telling the client in advance about past triumphs or sharing your testimonials and references *before* hassles occur has far more impact than doing it *after* there's a problem.

5. *Talk about the* work, *not your feelings or the process.*

Sometimes it's difficult, especially when you've worked so hard to learn your craft, to have a client basically ruin your efforts.

It's critical to focus on the product or service, not on your client's credentials, not on your client's attitude. Hard, but critical.

4. *Ask the obligating question.* "If I do *xxx*, will you be able to buy it then?" And make sure you list *everything* as part of the *xxx*.

I can't overemphasize the beauty and wonder of the obligating question. It forces the client or prospect to tell you what she really thinks. It forces her to focus. It gets all the issues on the table.

3. *Give the client lots of chances to give you negative* and *positive feedback.* Ask, "And what else?" a lot.

Back to the idea of asking questions. Of giving the prospect plenty of chances to talk. If you're like me, this isn't easy. But it's so powerful, so profitable, and so productive, you'll be glad you did it.

2. *Establish a written trail for everything.* Communicate *everything* by writing it down and send it to the client.

In this age of e-mail and fax, there's no excuse for not writing everything down. Get a reputation for it. Become a fiend about it. Your clients will thank you. So will your accountant.

When my wife and I tried to hire a contractor to do some work for us, four people came over. One took exhaustive notes. When we got the proposals, one was three times as long as the others and was filled with exhaustive detail.

Guess who we hired?

1. *Do your sale step by step.* Get their buy in, get them on your side.

You don't sell something all at once (unless it's a haircut or a hot dog). Instead, there are different steps you take people through, different stages of belief. The sooner you discover the stages, the sooner you'll make your sales calls more effective.

And one more thing: Always ask overt questions. What's an overt question? A clear, direct question that is designed to eliminate mutual misunderstandings.

LONTOS

Give the client lots of chances to give you negative *and* positive feedback

Pam Lontos has been training salespeople since 1981 as the owner of Lontos Sales and Motivation, Inc., of Orlando, Florida. And she says the biggest mistake salespeople make is talking too much. The problem, says Lontos, is that you don't get adequate feedback when you're providing too much output.

In her experience, salespeople need to provide less information, and ask more questions designed to elicit information. Questions like "What is your main concern?" and "Is there something you haven't told me?" will provide feedback about your client's positive and negative issues, she says. You can use that to help people feel you care about them and to help personalize your appeal.

So why be direct?

Few things are harder than asking someone for money. Maybe that's why so many people beat around the bush with their "management's assessment of competitive risks" and "there can be no assurance of success" mealymouthed platitudes. At least, that's the way Howard M. Getson sees it.

The president and cofounder of the software bootstrap IntellAgent Control Corporation has a way of courting investors that resembles a TV infomercial more than a typical prospectus. In one letter he sent to prospective investors, sentences like "now is a great time to invest" and "send in your subscription form today" stud the text like starbursts in a dull, overcast sky.

Does the directness of Getson's pyrotechnics work? He raised $6.8 million from 70 investors in two years.

Why is it so hard? We're trained to make inferences, not to be direct. It feels rude. It's not.

It's not rude? No. In the long run, it saves everyone time and money. You may encounter people who are taken aback by your direct approach. They might feel put upon or offended.

So why be direct? Because everyone perceives life differently. Overt questions clear the air, eliminating the he said/she said problem. If you and I saw an accident, no question that minutes later, you'd be reporting it to the police wrong! By using the overt question, we get rid of this mutual misunderstanding.

Need an example? Actually, here are a few:

- How much did you spend on promotional marketing last year?
- Do you like this?
- What three improvements can I make to this offer?
- Why?
- What specific information do you need to move ahead?
- What's a good example of what you're looking for?
- Is this project going well?

So what now? Make a list of the overt questions you need. In sales. In production. In marketing. There should be a basic set you can use over and over.

THE THREE REASONS PEOPLE DON'T BUY FROM YOU

Sometimes, even after you've done everything right (or you think you've done everything right), you still don't get the sale. Knowing what went wrong is important because it will help you do better next time. It turns out that almost every time you lose a sale, it's because of only three possible reasons.

1. *They don't trust you.* You're new in business, you're not dressed right, they don't like the way you shook hands, the brochure you've got is crummy, they heard you weren't honest, they heard from a friend that you don't do great work, your client list isn't very impressive, and you have a funny accent.

People buy when they believe that the product or service will make their lives better. And they don't believe if they can't trust the provider.

2. *They don't know what's in it for them.*

People don't usually buy drill bits. They buy holes.

If you do a poor job of communicating *exactly* how your product or service will benefit the prospect (not you, them), then you don't deserve to make the sale. Selling is about communication. Communicating benefits, communicating feeling.

One of the most frustrating things a bootstrapper faces is *knowing* that his product is better, cheaper, faster, or easier and being unable to sell it.

Ask yourself, "Would my mother buy this?" She trusts you (probably), but if she doesn't see the obvious benefit, she's not going to buy your product or service.

Think about the many, many things you've purchased. Why did you buy them? Usually, you can come up with a simple phrase—tasted good, made me look good, will make me healthier, it's fun. Yet most salespeople use very complicated, involved sales pitches.

Remember, the potential customer is thinking: "What's in it for me?"

3. *People rarely buy.* They're often sold.

You don't get the sale if they don't trust you

Richard Maradik is the CEO of Datamark, a direct-mail services company in Nashville. His office is a warehouse, and a particularly unimpressive one at that. So when prospects of the $3 million direct-mail company ask to meet him at his place of business, he might well make an excuse and suggest an alternative spot—such as one of Nashville's fancier restaurants.

Maradik, however, directs them to his warehouse—and then informs them of exactly what to expect. He even offers in advance to take them to dinner at a nearby McDonald's. Instead of putting people off, Maradik says his news disarms them. And prospects on a tight budget find it appealing that he's clearly so thrifty.

Queen Isabella didn't go out looking for someone to discover the New World. Columbus sold her on the journey. The American people didn't demand that JFK put a man on the moon—he sold the public on it.

People don't have to like being sold to end up liking what they buy.

You have a duty—to yourself, to your employees, to your shareholders, and most of all to your customers—to sell hard. You need to persist and you need to be clear. You must figure out how to overcome the fear that almost everyone feels when they buy something. Your clients will thank you for it.

Think this is overstated? Think about all the people with young kids who've died without life insurance because the salesperson couldn't teach the parents how important it was. Think about the patient who has emphysema because his doctor couldn't sell him on quitting smoking.

Don't you wish you'd bought tickets to that Dylan concert in '68? Or invested in the S&P 500 mutual fund in 1992?

Buying isn't about making a rational choice every time. So selling is about using emotion and logic together to help people buy things that will make their lives better.

THE FIVE THINGS YOU'D BETTER KNOW ABOUT COMPUTERS

1. Computers save you time, then they cost you time, then they save you time.

Simple uses of computers are a no-brainer for most companies. Using e-mail instead of faxes, for example, or word processing instead of typing. Many computer substitutions can quickly pay for themselves in time saved.

Faced with these obvious savings, companies often decide to take the next step. They decide to "computerize." This usually involves networking all the computers together. Creating management information systems. A paperless office. Complete online accounting and tax preparation. Almost always, computerization of your office is an expensive waste of time and money.

Why? Because entrepreneurs scrimp on the expense, forgetting about the cost. Hiring a great MIS (computer) person and buying the right hardware and software are investments. And if you try to do it yourself or be cheap about it, you've just added a new job to your ever-growing list—computer jock.

This is a painful transition for every company that tries it. Before you do, spend a lot of time with people in your business who have pulled it off. Then copy *exactly* what they did.

Only after doing this part of the process right will you earn the right to get to the third step—when computers start saving you money again. Like at *Fast Company* magazine, where they can build a magazine in 25 percent of the time it used to take. Or at Verifone, where no one writes memos, and employees can work in any country they please.

2. Just because you *can* do something with your computer doesn't mean you *should*.

This problem started when the Macintosh introduced lots of fonts. Suddenly, too many papers looked like ransom notes. For the past 12 years, you've been able to tell when a new feature is introduced into Microsoft Word, because lots of neophytes start using it right away. (Hint: You don't need to include drop caps in your business letters.)

Lately, my company has been focusing on getting back to basics. We use heavy paper, spiral binding, and tasteful fonts. We'll include a color photo in a presenta-

HEARTSONG

Kermit Heartsong sells education and games. But more, he sells family participation and parents' joy in playing learning games with their children.

After college, Heartsong invented a word game he used to help build his vocabulary. Then while working with disadvantaged youngsters as a volunteer in San Francisco, he found that the game helped them gain skills while they were having a good time. The discovery led him to found Quantum Gameworks, Inc., in 1990 with $40,000 in funds.

Heartsong markets more than 40 fun and educational games, half of them his invention and the rest licensed from other inventors. His customers are classy specialty retailers like the Nature Company and FAO Schwarz. But more rewarding for Heartsong are the daily letters and calls he gets from parents thanking him for giving them a way to enjoy learning with their children. What price can you put on that? About $4 million in sales a year, it turns out.

Help people buy things that will make their lives better

tion if we need it, but more than likely it's about the message, not the bells and whistles. The best book on this topic is Chuck Green's *Desktop Publisher's Idea Book*. Follow his instructions and you can't go wrong.

The same goes for the way you do your accounting. If you're busy doing regression analysis and tracking the variances in daily budget reports, you're probably missing the point. Simplicity in all things, especially accounting!

3. You're probably overlooking the number one use of your computer.

If I could keep just one function of my computer, there'd be no question what it would be: the address book. That's right. Not the spreadsheet or even the word processor.

My address book has more than 2,000 names in it. With notes about every person I've done business with or been referred to. There's no way I could keep this all in my head. Four years ago, I found a printer in Maryland who did a good job on some color postcards. Now I need postcards again, so I head to the address book. Boom, there he is.

Even better, the address book lets me track referrals and new business opportunities and maintain a "tickler file." If I approach someone for business in January who tells me that the new budgets start in May, you can bet that he gets a call from me on May 1.

Automating your memory is a spectacular benefit that computers offer you. Online address books allow you to dramatically leverage the most important part of your job—selling. They force you to follow the guerrilla mantra of consistency and persistence.

4. Back up everything, every day.

How much would you pay a terrorist to keep him from blowing up your computer and all the data in there? Guess what? If you don't start backing up, you *will* lose all your data. Maybe not today, maybe not tomorrow, but someday, and you may pay for the rest of your life. Computers and hard disks are expected to fail. Their developers even use the term "MTBF," or "mean (average) time before failure."

You can wish and hope, or you can buy yourself a tape drive or a recordable CD drive and start being serious about backing up. Yes, it's a pain. So what? It's worth it.

> 5. If it's a chore, it can probably be automated.

I can't tell you how frustrated I get seeing someone in my office manually addressing labels, or cutting and pasting documents to get them looking good, or filling out tax forms by hand.

Computers are very stupid, but they're very good at automation. If you can describe something you do over and over, then you can almost certainly teach a computer to do it for you.

Merging letters, for example, to past-due accounts. It will take you two hours to teach the computer to do this perfectly, and it will save you 30 minutes every week. Worth it? You bet.

Warning: Don't computerize something unless it's going to dramatically increase quality or pay for itself in three months or less. Otherwise, you're becoming a slave to a system that doesn't do you any good.

For example, I used to use TurboTax to do my taxes. After figuring out how much of my time it took to get the taxes into the computer, I discovered that my accountant could do it for less. He uses the same program, but he's better at it than I am. So I stopped buying TurboTax and use the time saved to make more sales, which makes me and the accountant very happy.

THE FOUR DOCUMENTS EVERY BOOTSTRAPPER NEEDS

As you build your business, you'll be creating value. That value will accrue to your brand name, your relationships with customers, the assets you buy, and the assets you build. You'll end up with a factory or systems or patents or something that's worth money.

When that happens, the fictional person called a corporation is suddenly worth something. Once you've got items of value, no doubt others will want a piece of that. For this reason, you've got to protect yourself. There are four things you can do right now that won't cost very much money but will pay off in a big way in the long run.

The first is an employee handbook. Even if you have just one employee, you'll want this bureaucratic document to be part of your hiring process. An employee handbook lays out the rules, the regulations, and, most important, the policies of your workplace. It can be a major step toward protecting you from a very expensive lawsuit.

To make it easier for you, I've included a sample. Please note that this is not a legal document and doesn't constitute legal advice. Instead, make the changes you think are appropriate and then show it to your lawyer for feedback. The important legal concept here is that you've got to treat employees fairly and within the law. By outlining your policies on everything from vacation to termination, you can make it more likely that you're covered.

You don't have to play around with many personal-information-management software packages to realize that PIMs are not very personal. The odds of finding one that exactly fits your personal needs are essentially nil. So don't bother, argues Jane Wesman, the president of the New York City bootstrap Jane Wesman Public Relations.

Wesman uses a bound notebook (looseleaf ones tend to lose pages) and a pen to manage the many details of author and book publicity tours. That's right, a paper notebook. On the first right-hand page she writes down what she has to do, prioritizing the first four or five items only, since that's all she's likely to get around to on any day. She leaves the left page blank to hold phone numbers, sticky notes, phone message slips, and the like. Every few days, she flips to a new page and starts over.

Simple, direct, and valuable—so valuable, that Wesman insists on most of her employees using the same system. And she won't let anyone's notebook leave the office, for fear of losing it.

Just because you can do some-thing doesn't mean you should

J. P. WHALEN

Automate your computer memory

J. P. Whalen doesn't like to phone sales prospects. But he does it, because his computer makes him. The president of the 14-year-old employee evaluation firm Human Resource Development Technologies in Wilmington, Delaware, has a database of 4,000 contacts built up through advertising, personal meetings, and other sources. And the contact management program he uses to organize it for direct mailings, telemarketing campaigns, tracking projects, and other things also automatically reminds him when he's scheduled to make follow-up calls to prospects.

Every morning when he boots up his computer, the program pops up a screen telling him whom to call and what about. Whalen's four-person staff doesn't include a marketing person, and he isn't planning to hire one anytime soon, despite his distaste for the task. Who needs it, when he has his computerized nag? "This is almost like having a sales manager sitting over my shoulder," he says, "saying this is something you must do."

YOUR COMPANY EMPLOYEE HANDBOOK

INTRODUCTION

This handbook is offered to give our employees a general description of work rules, benefits, and personnel policies of Your Company (YC). The handbook should not be construed as an employment contract or an agreement for employment for any specified period of time. YC reserves the right to make changes to this handbook as conditions require. When changes are necessary, you will be provided with supplements or a new handbook.

All paperwork necessary for your employment must be completed within one week from your date of hire. This includes federal and state tax forms, federal employment forms, and any others given to you.

TERMS OF EMPLOYMENT

Employment at Will

Your employment here is deemed Employment at Will, which means that you or the company can terminate your employment at any time with or without a reason or warning.

Copyright

We create valuable intellectual property. Everything that you create while working here is owned in full by YC, Inc., and no royalties or additional payments are due to any employee because of contributions made to this work. As a condition of your employment, you further warrant that everything you create here is original and, to the best of your knowledge, does not libel anyone or infringe on any copyrights.

Deductions

The law requires that the company deduct from your paycheck your federal income tax, state income tax, and Social Security tax. The amount of your check is your wages less such tax deductions and any other sums you authorize the company to deduct, such as medical insurance, savings plan, garnishments, and so on. These deductions are remitted to the proper agencies by the company. You should retain your check stub as a record of your earnings and deductions. You are responsible for confirming that the information listed there is correct.

Workers' Comp

If you should be injured at work, we provide Workers' Compensation insurance to cover your accident or injury. Any on-the-job injury must be reported to your supervisor as soon as it occurs.

If, by a doctor's recommendation, you must miss work because of a work-related injury, notify your supervisor. You may be eligible to receive weekly Workers' Compensation payments and medical treatment at no cost to you.

Social Security

Federal Social Security provides a variety of benefits, including retirement income, death benefits, disability benefits, and monthly income payments for certain dependent survivors of covered employees. A percentage of your gross earnings is deducted as your contribution for this protection. The company contributes an amount established by federal law. Normally, you will be eligible to receive a monthly income from Social Security when you retire or in the event that you become totally or permanently disabled.

Immigration

In compliance with the Immigration Reform and Control Act of 1986, we require all newly hired employees to present documented proof of identity and eligibility to work in the United States. Employees will be required to furnish this information within three working days of the hire date.

Dismissal

If your performance as an employee is unsatisfactory due to lack of ability or failure to fulfill the requirements of your job, you will be notified of the problem and your supervisor will work with you to correct the situation.

If this does not succeed, you will be dismissed. If you are dismissed, a full explanation of the reason will be given to you by your supervisor. We will take all steps necessary to work with an employee to correct or rectify a situation before taking the step of dismissal. If you believe you have been treated unfairly, you have the right to an interview with your superior.

Equal Opportunity

YC is an equal opportunity employer. In accordance with federal, state, and local laws, we recruit, hire, promote, and evaluate all personnel without regard to race, religion, color, sex, marital status, age, national origin, veteran status, disability, or any other personal characteristic protected by law, except where such characteristic is an appropriate bona fide occupational qualification. Job applicants and present employees are evaluated solely on ability, experience, and the requirements of the job.

PERSONNEL POLICIES

Feedback

All of us like to know how we're doing on the job. Day-by-day comments from supervisors help, but now and then there is a need to review all phases of your work performance.

Once a year you will receive a performance review. It's a procedure that requires each supervisor to evaluate the performance of every employee under his or her supervision. Your supervisor(s) will discuss your performance with you at the time of each performance review, point out how well you are carrying out your job, and suggest where and how improvements can be made. At this performance review, you will be able to discuss your compensation level.

The best way to get promoted is to find a task you want to do, persuade management to give you a chance to do it, then do it well. The best way to get a raise is to write down aggressive revenue-enhancing and profit-enhancing goals, share them with management, then reach them.

Outside Employment

It is expected that full-time employees' primary employment obligation is to YC, Inc. Therefore, any outside employment should not conflict with your job, your focus, or the scheduling of work shifts. We welcome outside interests on your part, be they community activities, second jobs, or school. While we will do everything possible to accommodate you, please understand that your primary commitment must be to our projects. Anything that you do outside the office should not affect your energy, enthusiasm, or input to your work here, nor should it conflict with our corporate goals.

Do not use company time or equipment (even after hours) for personal work. Doing so has all sorts of tax and legal liability implications for you, as well as for this company.

Clients

We encourage our clients to have extensive interactions with us. We also encourage you to take initiative with clients. Part of the basis of this trust is that we ask our clients not to solicit our employees to leave here, and it is inappropriate for you to ask any client you work with directly about job opportunities. This makes us appear unprofessional, and it takes advantage of the company's investments in client relationships.

Privacy

Other people's computers, company files, and documents are off limits. Rooting through other people's personal files is grounds for dismissal. In general, you should not have

HANK'S ROOT BEER

You must believe in your product

Bill Dunman's friends told him he was crazy to start a soft-drink company. So what? Every bootstrapper hears that. But Dunman's friends were all long-time employees of the Coca-Cola Company, where he worked for 11 years before cofounding Hank's Root Beer Company of Philadelphia.

Their main point: Coke and Pepsi basically divide the beverage market between them, leaving scarcely a six-pack for the rest of the soft-drink companies to survive on. Both are remarkably sophisticated behemoths, known for marketing savvy, octopus-like distribution, relentless competitive drive, and ironclad customer loyalty. And these were the people from whom Dunman would have to steal market share.

Not to worry, the ex-Coke man said. "People are looking for something other than Coke or Pepsi." And his belief has been validated as Hank's sales have mounted nearly $2 million a year. More important, Dunman's belief in his product is still growing.

private materials on your computer. If you need to create something you'd rather not share, please take it home on a floppy disk.

The privacy edict applies to management, but not when it comes to passwords or looking for files in your absence. If there's something on your machine you don't want management to see, take it off your machine. That's the only way to ensure that the organization has access to your files when needed.

Harassment

It is the policy of the company to maintain a working environment free from all forms of unlawful harassment or intimidation. This includes all forms of unwelcome sexual advances, requests for sexual favors, and other verbal or physical conduct of a sexual nature, all of which are serious violations of our policy and will not be condoned or permitted. Not only is unlawful harassment a violation of our policy, but it may also violate federal and state law. Any employee who is subjected to unlawful harassment or intimidation should contact the company president's office. All complaints of unlawful harassment will be promptly investigated in a confidential manner to the extent practical. Any employee, manager, or supervisor who violates this policy will be subject to appropriate disciplinary action up to and including discharge. Furthermore, any employee who brings forward a legitimate complaint may not be retaliated against.

Hours, Full and Flex

A full-time regular employee is an employee who works a standard workweek, in accordance with a schedule determined upon hiring. Such an employee is paid a monthly salary, and it is expected that when projects require additional time, this will be provided by the employee with no overtime pay due.

A part-time employee is one who works an irregular schedule, by the hour and/or project, to be determined upon hiring. These employees submit their hours to their supervisors for payment once a month, prior to regular check-cycle scheduling.

Health insurance, vacation, holiday, and paid sick days are not available for part-time employees.

BENEFITS

Vacation

After you have been employed for 6 months, you will receive 5 paid vacation days.

Each regular employee will be entitled to 10 paid vacation days in the second year of employment, and 15 days thereafter.

Vacation time is based on a calendar year. Vacation time may not be carried over from one year to the next.

KITCHEN BUSINESS

Don't do anything you wouldn't tell your mother about

Milton Gralla and his brother started their publishing business with $20,000 and a philosophy: "Live on the give, not on the take, and you will get rich and stay rich." That was in 1955; their first publication, a trade journal called *Kitchen Business*, was successful enough to provide the foundation for a publishing company that 28 years later would include 20 magazines.

Behind it all, says Milton Gralla, now a bestselling author, was the same philosophy that nice guys finish first. The Grallas kept promises, treated employees fairly, and bent over backward to help customers. That included more than giving good service. Gralla recalls telling one regional company not to advertise in nationally distributed *Kitchen Business* because it wasn't a good use of funds. Instead, he recommended a direct-mail campaign. The grateful would-be advertiser referred far more business to Gralla than he'd have gotten by taking the money.

And, by the way, the nice guys definitely finished toward the front of the pack. When the Grallas sold their publishing company in 1983, it brought $73 million.

If an employee quits voluntarily without giving the company at least one week's notice, he or she is not entitled to any paid vacation. If a person is discharged by the company, he or she is entitled to payment for any accrued vacation time.

Holidays

We have seven paid holidays, which we observe as follows: New Year's Day, Memorial Day, Independence Day, Labor Day, Thanksgiving Day and the following Friday, and Christmas Day.

In addition, one floating day can be taken for miscellaneous holidays such as Yom Kippur, St. Patrick's Day, or Ramadan.

Personal Time

Regular employees may take up to two personal days off per calendar year, subject to scheduling such days in a way that does not interfere with the company's ability to meet its deadlines.

Sick Leave

Regular employees may take up to five sick days per year. In unusual circumstances when an employee needs additional sick days, he or she must discuss the situation with the employer.

Maternity/Family Leave

Leave will be offered with pay for the first four weeks and without pay for up to eight subsequent weeks to eligible employees (must have worked for YC at least one year) for the following reasons:

*   maternity leave for birth mother
*   care of a seriously ill spouse, child, or parent
*   an employee's own serious health condition that prevents the employee from performing his or her job
*   adoption or foster care within the first 12 months of the placement
*   care of a child in the first 12 months after birth (father only)

See your supervisor if you need a leave of absence for any reason not covered under this policy.

Health Insurance

The company will pay for primary health care coverage for every full-time employee under the basic insurance plan of the company's choosing. The employee can arrange for additional medical coverage for dependents to be deducted directly from his or her pay on a pretax basis. An employee becomes eligible for coverage on the first of the month

VULCAN LEAD

Work expands to fill the available space

Chuck Yanke has bootstrapped more businesses than most people ever dream of, and he knows the demands of starting and running a small business. One of the requirements of successful bootstrapping is knowing when to give in to those demands and when to turn them over to somebody else. "You only have twenty-four hours in a day and occasionally your wife does like to see you," reasons Yanke.

The CEO of 60-person Vulcan Lead Products in Milwaukee uses something with the fancy name of the Pareto principle to decide how he's going to spend the hours he has to give to work. You probably know the Pareto principle as the 80-20 rule, which states that 80 percent of results are usually caused by 20 percent of causes. That's true whether you're talking about profits or absenteeism.

Using the Pareto principle in bootstrapping is largely a matter of deciding which is the 20 percent that's causing the trouble or creating the profit. And that's where you decide to spend the time you have to give to work. "It's amazing the number of times that old eighty-twenty rule lets you sift through the BS," says Yanke. "Whatever's important rises to the top."

following 30 days of employment. If you decline coverage at the start of your employment, you will not be eligible to join until the anniversary of the start of the plan, which occurs every April, unless there is a specific qualifying event that supersedes this rule.

Bonuses

Because of the unpredictable nature of our business, the bonus policy is subject to annual adjustments. Therefore, see the attached, dated document for the current bonus plan.

Expenses

You will be reimbursed for all reasonable expenses you incur in the performance of your job. Any expense over $100 must have the prior approval of a supervisor. You must submit original receipts for all items that the company will pay for. This applies both to items charged on any company credit card for which YC will issue a check, and also to any expenses for which you will be reimbursed directly.

If you are using an account for which the company will be billed directly, you must obtain the necessary approvals and submit receipts. If you are using a company card that is in your own name or your own personal credit card, you must still get prior verbal approvals for charges over $100, and submit all receipts with your expense voucher for reimbursement.

Miscellaneous

Telephone, Messenger Services, Fedex, UPS, E-mail
- Limit your personal calls to 10 minutes a day or less.
- If you make long distance calls, please reimburse. Our phone bill is a *lot* bigger than yours.
- Limit your personal e-mail use to a reasonable amount.
- If you must use messenger services, Fedex, UPS, or other office resources for personal reasons, you must reimburse YC.

Computers

You and only you are responsible for backing up every single piece of data you depend on. We provide a network backup. In addition, you should back up your most crucial files yourself to avoid any possibility of loss of work.

Dress Code

No pajamas. Nothing ripped. Nothing (too) revealing. Need we say more?

PENNY'S PASTRIES

As you grow, the cash crunch starts to get serious

When Southwest Airlines decided to serve Penny McConnell's cookies on its flights, the order amounted to a year's worth of sales for Penny's Pastries—every month. It sounded like the dream she'd been pursuing ever since she'd started selling cookies she'd baked in her own oven.

It turned into a nightmare. The huge order overwhelmed her eight-person bootstrap. She borrowed heavily for equipment, supplies, employees, and a larger facility. She cut prices to fit Southwest's budget. When quality problems cropped up, costs ballooned and big profits turned to huge losses. Six months after shipping the first Southwest order, Penny's Pastries filed for bankruptcy.

What happened? Too much of a good thing. "It was just a tremendous increase in volume," she says. Now back in business, McConnell won't bake a cookie for any customer until she knows she can do it profitably.

Housekeeping and Cleanliness

Everyone is responsible for keeping the office clean.

Parking

Our company provides free parking facilities. However, we cannot be liable for fire, theft, damage, or personal injury involving employees' automobiles. Protect your property by locking your car doors. Courtesy and common sense in parking and driving will help you avoid accidents, personal injuries, and damage to your car and to those of others. No overnight parking is allowed.

Smoking

No smoking is permitted in the office. Smoking breaks are not permitted.

The second document every bootstrapper needs is an umbrella insurance policy. This is a fairly inexpensive policy that covers your liability from a whole host of lawsuits. You can get a million or more dollars' worth of coverage for less than you might think. It can cover you over and beyond the maximum coverage of your other insurance policies—for protection against a catastrophic claim.

The third document is a freelancer agreement. It is used for all the people who work for you who aren't your employees. More and more bootstrappers are recognizing that freelancers are more flexible, easier to hire and fire, and, sometimes, less expensive than full-time employees. But as Microsoft learned when it was sued by a group of consultants and freelancers, things are not always as straightforward as they seem.

First, if you're hiring full-time people and calling them freelancers to save on taxes, think again. The IRS eagerly pursues this tax dodge, and sooner or later, you're going to get caught. The IRS document #SS-8 lists the standards someone must meet to be considered a freelancer under the law.

While there are countless folks who have avoided being hassled by the IRS, using this test is a great way (but by no means a guaranteed way) to avoid a huge tax bill. Microsoft, for example, ended up paying legal fees and penalties, plus awarding stock options and other benefits to hundreds of people.

So the first third of the document you need to use in working with freelancers does two things: It outlines the IRS policy. And it states that both you and the freelancer believe you're following the policy. While the ultimate distinction is up to your friendly auditor, this can be an important piece of the paper trail in your defense.

The second part of the document is a work-for-hire agreement. Let's say you hire a freelancer to create a logo for you. And then you hit the big time. One day, the designer shows up and demands a license fee for the logo you've been using all

TYSON

Corporations have developed very sophisticated ways of managing cash, from equipment leasing to factoring. But John Tyson proved that cash management doesn't mean you have to get fancy.

When Tyson was struggling to make a living hauling chickens from Arkansas farms to cities such as Chicago and Houston, he'd get gas stations along his route to let him fill up on credit. On the return, after selling his cargo of poultry, he'd pay off the stations with cash.

And Tyson innovated in other ways, installing feed and water systems on his truck to sustain chickens on long journeys to market, for instance. Tyson's approaches helped nourish a company that today is the world's largest chicken concern, with annual sales topping $6 billion.

Don't spend money until you get money

these years. Sure, you've already paid for it. But the law is a little fuzzy regarding copyright and related issues. Fortunately, there's a straightforward way to keep everything clear.

A work-for-hire agreement simply says that all the work created for you belongs to you. That your onetime payment entitles you to exploit the work in any way you choose. Did you know, for example, that most photographers keep the copyright in the photos they take? That's right. If you hire a photographer to take a publicity photo of you and your partner, it doesn't belong to you unless you specifically get a work-for-hire letter signed.

Some freelancers won't sign a work-for-hire letter as a matter of principle. That's fine. Our principle says that we hire a different freelancer.

The last part of the agreement covers shared work and trade secrets. Many of the freelancers who work for you will be developing their skills as they do work for you. That's great—it's part of the deal, and it helps create a community of talented resource people when their experiences go into the mix. But that's different from having a freelancer use the actual underlying work you paid for to help a competitor.

You also want to include a nondisclosure agreement. This prohibits freelancers from using internal corporate information to help them in other areas. It prohibits them, for example, from walking down the street and selling their services to your competitor, based on what they know about how you run your business. Nondisclosure agreements are extremely hard to enforce (and almost never worth what they cost to enforce). But in my experience, just informing a freelancer in writing that you consider things confidential is enough to forestall any problems.

Most people mean well. They come to work with you with no malice, and virtually every engagement works out fine. But these precautions do two things for you. First, they clearly communicate what you expect. After all, misunderstandings

YOGEN FRÜZ

When Aaron and Michael Serruya approached several US frozen-yogurt store chains about obtaining franchise rights in their native Canada, they were told to be patient—Canadian expansion wouldn't happen for a year or so. The brothers, then 19 and 20, decided that meant they had a competition-free year in which to bootstrap their own Canadian yogurt store. They leaped into action.

Backed with a loan from their father, plus proceeds from the sale of Aaron's part-ownership in a bagel shop, they bootstrapped their own yogurt store. The first Yogen Früz frozen-yogurt shop opened in a Toronto mall in 1986, and the brothers—later joined by younger brother Simon—were inundated with requests from potential franchisees. They were only too happy to oblige, and today are global leaders in the frozen yogurt industry, with more than 3,500 franchised and company-owned stores.

Run circles around the competition

cause most problems. And second, if something does spiral out of hand, they give you a first line of defense that might scare away a contingency fee lawyer out for a quick buck.

The last document is the most controversial, but it's also the one I feel the most strongly about. It's not even a document. It's a no-lawyer paragraph. It says this:

> Any disagreements about the interpretation of this agreement will be settled through informal binding arbitration, to be conducted by a mutually acceptable arbitrator.

That's it. What's it mean? It means that in every contract you sign with anyone— employees, customers, suppliers, whatever—both parties agree to forget the lawyers. It means that, faced with a dispute, both sides have to work it out, or face swift and certain justice at the hands of an arbitrator.

The reason is simple: The threat of a lawsuit can freeze everything. It can ruin your business and consume your life. It takes your eye off the ball and changes the focus of your day.

When there isn't an arbitration clause, it's very easy to threaten a lawsuit. And if you're dealing with someone who might be crazy enough to go through with it, you've got to take the threat seriously. Basically, you've armed yourself and your counterpart with nuclear weapons. "I don't care if I wipe myself out—you're going with me."

One of the most successful projects I ever worked on was marred by a situation like this. There were four parties involved, and as long as all four could work together, we were making lots of money and having great fun. Then, two of the parties decided that they wanted a bigger piece of the pie.

They hired a lawyer. Threatened to issue press releases. Threatened to end the entire project unless my partner and I paid them blackmail money. Now, these

TRAVELER'S

J. G. Batterson had just begun his insurance business when a banker accosted him at the local post office. What would it take, the man asked, to insure him against an accident for a trip from there to home, where lunch was waiting? Two cents, Batterson replied, and slipped the coins into his pocket.

And that is how the Traveler's insurance company got its start, as a bootstrap operation back in 1864. The two pennies, by the way, are reportedly still in the till at Traveler's headquarters in Hartford, Connecticut.

Give clients a safe, reliable way to leverage your fearlessness

people were crazy. I knew it and they knew it. I also knew that we would win in court if it came to that.

But court would have cost us at least $200,000 and taken years. In the meantime, the golden goose would have died. So we hired the most expensive, scariest lawyer we could. He wrote some withering letters to the other side and then charged us $7,000 (for three letters!). The other side was softened up but was still facing $10,000 in their own legal bills.

As we continued to talk about settling this nonissue, the golden egg laid a lot fewer eggs. But as with most lawsuits, this one just petered out. Everyone got tired and went away.

A pain in the neck. A windfall for the lawyers. And the good guys didn't win (they never do in court).

Here's how it might have worked if we had insisted on the informal arbitration clause:

1. The crazy folks announce they're going to sue.

2. We point out that there's an arbitration clause, and gladly agree to go to arbitration.

3. They pick a lawyer. We pick a lawyer. The two lawyers agree on an arbitrator.

4. The arbitrator allows each side to write a three-page memo defending their point of view, and to suggest a settlement.

5. The arbitrator must then pick one settlement or the other.

Faced with this alternative, the would-be blackmailers realize that their complaint is nothing. The issue quickly disappears.

Ask any lawyer about arbitration. She'll start by telling you that it's a bad idea

Consider selling directly

When Mary Kay Ash ran across a woman who made an excellent skin cream in her home, she could have bought the rights to the cream and tried to convince retailers to carry it. Instead, she took $5,000 and an idea and started a new kind of business. Her plan was to get carefully trained saleswomen to demonstrate a line of skin care products to small groups of women in their homes.

By selling directly, Ash was able to control the pricing, distribution, and quality of her product from the beginning. Did it work? Sales the first year, when she had only nine so-called beauty consultants working for her, were $200,000. By the next year, they'd topped $800,000.

Twenty-five years later, there were 475,000 beauty consultants around the world, sales were over $2 billion, and Mary Kay's pink Cadillacs had become a cultural icon.

Cut out the middle-man

It used to be that consumers bought from retailers, who bought from distributors, who bought from manufacturers, who actually produced the goods. Then along came Sam Walton, who in 1962 started a retail chain that acted as its own distributor.

It may not sound like much, but most observers agree that savvy Sam's integration of a distribution system with a discount store chain is what propelled Wal-Mart to the top spot among the world's retailers. It helped in two ways. First, Sam saved on the middleman markup slapped on by wholesalers and distributors. That let him cut prices to shoppers while maintaining adequate profit margins. Second, he was better able to keep his stores stocked with what was selling, when it was selling. That kept people coming in while it reduced his inventory costs.

The Wal-Mart system is highly sophisticated, extremely cost-conscious, and, some would say, ruthlessly competitive. But that's not why Wal-Mart went from one store in Rogers, Arkansas, to 3,000 stores worldwide and over $100 billion in annual sales. The explanation for that is easy: It was Walton's simple solution of cutting out the middleman.

There's always room for inno-vation

The last time anybody came up with a new pen was 1963, when felt-tip markers began to challenge the ballpoints that had held sway over fountain pens since the 1930s. In other words, the writing implement is not exactly a promising field for innovation. But that didn't stop Jamesen Saviano from coming up with a new idea.

The 12-year-old from Norwalk, Connecticut, noticed that when he and other students were learning to write, they often pressed down too hard, sometimes even ripping the paper. So he invented a writing accessory that uses magnets to control the pushing force of the tip of a pen or pencil against a surface. Press too hard, and it comes apart. Lift up, the magnets rejoin.

Jamesen's idea for the LiteRite writing aid hasn't made a bootstrapper of him yet. But it was enough to land him a patent and win an invention award from a national retailer—as well as prove that there's no such thing as no room for a new idea.

(no surprise!). But when pressed, she'll probably admit that the little company without resources for lawyers usually comes out ahead by using arbitration.

True story: My company's new lawyer, one of the most respected in New York City, just made us sign an agreement that requires arbitration if we have an argument with the firm. That's right. Arbitration chosen by a law firm. Why? It made their malpractice premium go down.

THE TEN BOOTSTRAPPER COMMANDMENTS

The most common question would-be entrepreneurs ask me isn't really a question at all. It's a plea for knowledge, a fear of the unknown: "I'm almost ready to start my own business. But what do I need to know before I start?"

Here, for the first time anywhere, are the Ten Bootstrapper Commandments. A Cliff Notes version of the big stuff you'd better know before taking the plunge.

FIRST COMMANDMENT: BE AUDACIOUS

You have less to lose than you think. In fact, compared to almost anyone else on the planet, you have very little to lose indeed.

Sure, you might have to get a job. Maybe it will take you a little while to get back to entrepreneuring. But you're not going to starve, nor is it likely you'll

Vital vision

The name of Harry Gottlieb's bootstrap is more of a play on television than on entrepreneurial vision, but the fact is, the founder's vision of interactive education and entertainment is perhaps the most important asset possessed by Chicago-based Jellyvision. Jellyvision is best known for its You Don't Know Jack line of interactive trivia-game software. And You Don't Know Jack is best known for its wisecracking, edgy attitude.

What's less known is Gottlieb's past as an award-winning producer of educational films and his (projected) future as an architect of a whole new medium. In fact, everything Gottlieb does is based on what he calls his Jack principles—namely, to keep choices limited, to maintain a rapid pace, to give users one task at a time, and to use spoken output to guide users instead of only on-screen cues. The vision guides not only the Jack games but also a slew of future projects, from interactive news programs to Jack-like investment guides, which Gottlieb has in the works.

So do you think being a visionary is unrewarding? If so, consider that Gottlieb has sold a million copies of the $30 Jack games since 1995.

lose your house—unless you did no planning before you started!

The main advantage that bootstrappers have over everyone else is audacity. They are willing to be thinner, quicker, smarter, and more flexible than their big company cousins.

Push your productive audacity to the limit. Stay just this side of foolishness.

At age 16, I started a ski club in my high school. My competition was the most popular physical education teacher in the school. I had no chance to succeed. He got to promote his club to every one of his classes. I was prohibited from even posting a flyer.

Fortunately, I was too motivated and too foolish to realize that it was a hopeless cause. So I did it. And I did audaciously. I focused on word of mouth. I focused on being small but flexible. I charged more, so I could attract the kids who wanted the "best" ski club. And I did something that no one had ever tried before—I ran the club on Friday nights instead of Wednesdays.

By confounding all the conventional wisdom, my club stood out. It also made some money and lasted long enough that I could pass it on to my sister when I went off to college.

Are you audacious? If not, better find a partner who is—or keep your day job.

SECOND COMMANDMENT: BE CHEAP

Money is a funny thing. You don't really know just how important it is until you need it.

The challenge of being cheap is to do it while not compromising things that really matter. If you don't get many visitors in your office, buy the cheapest furniture

KOO'S

Slow and steady wins the race

When Yul Ku came to Los Angeles from Korea in 1975, he went to work as a sewing machine operator to pay the rent. After three years of working and saving, he opened a 3,200-square-foot garment factory called Koo's Manufacturing. He treated his mostly immigrant workforce fairly, resisted the trend to move to lower-cost regions or countries, and specialized in turning around orders quickly.

Slowly and steadily, Ku grew. He never borrowed too much, limited expansion to moving to a modestly larger facility every few years, was always willing to look into new technology, and—critically—never gave up equity in the company. He didn't grow as fast as some, but neither did he go broke or lose control to investors, as many others have.

And today he is the sole owner of a 240,000-square-foot factory where 1,000 people make 90,000 pairs of pants a week, primarily for the Gap and Calvin Klein. Estimated annual sales for Koo's have grown slowly and steadily to over $115 million.

in the world. If you don't need business cards very often, skip them. If you can get by with a used computer and the software that came with it, fine.

It's *your* money. Treat it that way.

Once you've spent some time trying to book sales, you'll discover that money is hard to come by. You'll realize that a motivated, pleasant customer with cash in hand is a lot more attractive than a big maybe. And once you see how much money is worth when you're selling, you'll probably become a much better buyer.

You see, salespeople are the best customers. They understand that making a quick yes or no decision is great for both people. And they know how to describe what they want to buy.

Spend every dollar like it was your last one. Be really clear about what the money is for, demand perfection, and then pay your bills. You'll build a loyal cadre of suppliers. And you'll have money to build your business.

THIRD COMMANDMENT: ENJOY THE RIDE

After 12 years of full-time bootstrapping, I can tell you that every day is different from the one before. The projects change, the challenges change, and the people change. The ever-churning landscape is one reason that bootstrappers find the process so exciting.

At the same time, though, the issues never seem to change. I worry as much about money now as I did when it was just me in my house. I have the same hassles, the same challenges, the same moments of stress.

At the beginning, I believed that once this happened or once that happened, then everything would change. First, the goal was a $10,000 sale. It seemed unattainable. I knew that once I hit it, I'd be on easy street. Then it was a $100,000 sale. That, I was sure, would change everything. The stress would go away, clients would be calling me asking for new products—the whole nine yards.

Then, of course, it was the $500,000 sale. Well, we've gotten a few of those and they seem awfully similar to those $10,000 sales. The process is the same, the work is similar—it's just the teams that are bigger.

If you're not enjoying the ride at the beginning, you're never going to like it. Focusing on what's really important and handling that should be part of your daily ritual.

Most bootstrappers are so talented that they could make more money in a corporate job. So don't fool yourself into thinking that this is a temporary situation and you're doing it for the money. It's not and you're not. Do it for the process. Life's a journey. Enjoy it.

FOURTH COMMANDMENT: DON'T BELIEVE EVERYTHING YOU READ

There are three things I'd encourage you to avoid believing.

The first is business books. Even this one. No one is smart enough to know all the answers. If they were, I can promise you they wouldn't be writing those answers down for you! Books are a great foundation. They can outline the important questions. They can fill you with confidence. They can even give you enough examples to draw your own conclusions about what you ought to do.

But your situation is different. It always is. So be prepared to improvise. Be prepared to do exactly what the book tells you not to do, as long as it makes sense in your situation.

Second, avoid believing the trend analyses and analysts and pundits who are quick to tell you about what the world will be like in five years. They don't have a clue. And building an entire business around a prediction is a scary thing indeed.

Do some people get rich with the latest trend? No doubt about it. Think of all those Internet entrepreneurs who were in the right place at the right time. Proof that trend monitoring works. But for every Geocities and every Lycos there are a dozen companies that have utterly failed.

You're much more likely to make a great living—or even a fortune—by fulfilling basic human needs. The key is finding a niche in which you're satisfying a need *and* making money.

The third thing is the most important to ignore. And also the hardest. It's the media. Particularly, the media's coverage of entrepreneurial wunderkinds. Folks who start with nothing and become billionaires, seemingly with no effort. Phil Knight, Jerry Yang, Barry Diller, and dozens of other business celebrities make it look easy as they jet from meeting to meeting and deal to deal. Of course, the media don't bother to tell you about all the rejections these stars faced, all the near misses and close calls each dealt with along the way.

In building your business, you're likely to compare yourself to these titans. Like an iceberg, most of whose mass is below the water's surface, most bootstrappers toil in relative obscurity, creating top-quality work and making a decent living—but never lunching at the Four Seasons or doing deals by the pool.

FIFTH COMMANDMENT: DEVELOP GOOD HABITS

When you start your business, you'll adopt some patterns that will stay with you throughout your career. If you set up these patterns right from the start, you'll find that they're easy to stick with and will help you create lasting value. On the other hand, if you start off in a panic, lurching from crisis to crisis, you'll never develop the foundation you'll need.

PIZZA HUT

The model makes it work

Frank and Dan Carney had never cooked a pizza when they signed the lease for their first pizza restaurant. Only Frank had ever tasted what was, in 1950s Wichita, an almost unknown dish. Neither had restaurant experience, and their capital amounted to $600 from their late father's life insurance.

When they opened the first Pizza Hut in 1958, the ramshackle restaurant became a post-football game rendezvous for students at nearby Wichita State University. The two brothers were trying to go to college while running their bootstrap, but they also wanted to expand what had become a four-store chain.

The model they selected was franchising, and for the next several years they grew rapidly—and uncontrollably. Quality suffered as franchisees did whatever they wanted in the way of formulating ingredients, designing menus, and decorating restaurants. Beginning in 1961, the Carneys instituted firm controls on everything from architecture to recipes. Their pioneering refinements to franchising helped make Pizza Hut one of the archetypal restaurant success stories. By 1977, the year the Carneys sold the chain to Pepsico, there were more than 2,000 Pizza Hut restaurants.

GT BICYCLES

Not long after Gary Turner turned his skills as a trumpet repairman and race car driver to building a new frame for his son's mountain bike, he found himself making frames for every kid in their Fullerton, California, neighborhood. But it took a chance meeting with an Anaheim bike shop owner, Richard Long, for his avocation to become anything more.

What Long contributed was the ability to see biking as a business and the capital he raised by selling his shop. The two set up a company called GT Bicycles—using Turner's initials—in 1979 and soon made a name for their sturdy, high-quality machines. Success continued to the point that GT commanded more than a third of the youth bike market, and their bikes were even ridden in the Olympics.

The company went public in 1995. Long died in an accident in 1996, but Turner remains active in the company. Their collaboration now garners more than $700 million a year.

Two minds are better than one

The first habit is kindness. Make it a habit to return every phone call and answer every e-mail. Make it a habit to be nice to all of your contacts, regardless of their position in an organization. Make it a habit to say nothing if you can't say something nice.

In a world where people have countless options about whom to work with and how much to pay for the privilege, the importance of being nice isn't surprising. People remember kindness for a long, long time.

The second habit is learning. Read as much as you can. Read trade journals and business books and even business history. Go to seminars and trade shows and peer groups. If you allocate just an hour a day to learning about the outside world and your market, you'll probably be about 55 minutes a day ahead of your competition.

The third habit is publicity. Every time you make a sale, send out a press release. Every chance you get to give a speech, give one. Join the chamber of commerce or your industry's trade group. Send a monthly newsletter to everyone in your Rolodex, outlining what you're up to.

At first, this will feel funny. It's not something your mom taught you to do. But like all habits, you'll get used to it. And once you do, it'll not only feel natural, it will become profitable. And once it's profitable, you'll never stop!

The fourth habit is record keeping. If you start throwing your receipts in a shoe box, you'll probably never stop. On the other hand, a simple record-keeping system used from day one is easy to maintain and invaluable.

Don't just keep records for your taxes. Also keep careful records of prospects and clients, along with a log of whom you've contacted and when. And a scrapbook of important moments in your company's history—you'll be amazed at how fast you forget the good stuff when you're in the middle of a crisis.

All four habits won't take you very long. But they'll pay dividends over and over again.

SIXTH COMMANDMENT: MAKE MISTAKES

Big companies hate to make mistakes. They have a lot of trouble placing blame, and they don't like to be in the position of rewarding failure. This is a huge plus for a bootstrapper. As a bootstrapper, you can take risks and make mistakes and get away with them. Why? Because few mistakes are fatal, and the learning they create is significant. Even better, the risk-taking attitude behind them leads to countless market opportunities that a risk-averse person would never encounter.

Of course, bootstrappers don't like making mistakes, either. When it's your money, a mistake seems even more scary—your company is at stake. And that's a hurdle you'll have to overcome.

Some of the worst moments in my bootstrapping career have come from living with my mistakes. At the same time, it's crystal clear to me that without mistakes, I would have been out of business a long time ago. Why? Because so many of my "mistakes" turned into solid businesses.

You need to measure your mistakes, write them down, and reward yourself for them. If you can go a whole week without making a mistake, you're not trying hard enough!

SEVENTH COMMANDMENT: SEEK PROFESSIONAL HELP

Every successful bootstrapper recognizes that she can't do everything well. She knows that she's competing against bigger, stronger, smarter organizations that have the resources to hire some great people.

If you have a legal question, ask the smartest, most expensive lawyer you can find. If you need accounting help, get someone who's perfect for the job. Obviously, you don't need F. Lee Bailey to help you fight the zoning board, but skimping on professionals is a sure way to waste money.

Hothouse boot- strappers

One of the best places a bootstrapper can roost is in an entrepreneurial incubator. These business-boosting organizations select promising ventures and provide low-cost office space and services, professional advice, and proximity to other high-energy and high-risk enterprises. The mix is a nourishing one.

Take the case of Katherine Hammer and Evolutionary Technologies International, which the former linguist cofounded to make and market data integration solutions for large companies. When Hammer hooked up with one local incubator in Austin, Texas, she was taken in hand by entrepreneur George Kozmetsky, the cofounder of Teledyne, Inc. An early investor to the tune of $250,000 was Admiral Bobby Inman, the former head of the Microelectronics and Computer Technology Corporation high-tech consortium. Other investors ponied up $1.25 million more.

Best of all for Hammer and her partner, they didn't have to give up control to get their bootstrap off the ground. Only in the third round of financing did they have to relinquish even majority ownership. Today they preside over a company with 170 employees and sales of over $22 million.

LANCE RAKE

Lance Rake conceived of ergonomically designed playing cards as something senior citizens with arthritis would cotton to. It was only after the University of Kansas industrial design professor had bootstrapped the New Deal Playing Card Company into existence that he discovered a more appealing deal: kids.

Children would pick up his Ergo Cards and take to them immediately, Rake found. He reasoned that youngsters have trouble learning to shuffle, and his cards, featuring wavelike shapes that fit smoothly into the hand, made the trick easier. So he came out with Kid Cards, which are the same product with more colorful backs printed on them. New Deal, of Leawood, Kansas, notched $125,000 in first-year sales and projected $1 million for its second year, driven largely by the Kid Cards.

Change direction when the market tells you to

The best time to find professionals is *before* you need them. Ask around. Interview people. Develop relationships with the real professionals so they'll be available when you need them. The time to find help with your taxes is not the day after the IRS calls.

The flip side (why is there always a flip side?) is that the professionals will almost always overestimate the importance of their profession to your business. So you get to decide when to call in the professionals. Never write them a blank check.

EIGHTH COMMANDMENT: PUT YOUR PLAN IN WRITING

The theater is a great place for improvisation. On the other hand, business is an expensive place to make things up as you go along.

Most bootstrappers don't have a written plan because they don't know what to write. They're afraid to commit themselves to hard decisions, fearful that a written commitment to a plan can lead to failure later on.

Successful bootstrappers realize that you're going to have to make these decisions someday anyway, so you might as well make them before you start spending money, before you have deadlines, before you face a crisis.

Make a business plan. A marketing plan. A cash-flow plan. A hiring plan. A plan for the future. Write it down. It doesn't have to be great, but it does have to be in writing. Then add your goals—personal and professional. Some of what you write may be painful. Some of it will undoubtedly be boring. But all of it will lay a foundation for your continued success.

NINTH COMMANDMENT: CHARGE FOR YOUR TIME

Your most valuable asset is your time. Figure out what it's worth, and charge yourself for it.

Once you discover that you're spending $200 of your time to argue about a $10 parking ticket, you'll get a lot more efficient about your time. Once you discover that a bookkeeper can save you $500 a week in profitable selling time, you're more likely to hire a bookkeeper.

Bootstrappers don't spend a lot of time in meetings. So we end up with long, uninterrupted streaks of productive time. Sometimes, this productivity is seductive. We discover just how much we can get done in front of a laptop.

You want to install your own software, install your own phone service, carefully compare different online services to pick just the right one. Instead, *focus*. Spend your core time, your productive time on the tasks with the highest leverage. Once you're making money, you're entitled to have some fun and crawl around installing phone jacks. Until then, get someone cheaper to do everything you can delegate.

TENTH COMMANDMENT: REMEMBER WHERE YOU CAME FROM

For every wannabe bootstrapper, there are 10 or 20 success stories. People who have managed to turn the corner and build successful, sustainable, profitable businesses.

Once you cross the threshold from bootstrapper to businessperson, a funny thing happens. You quickly forget all the wrong turns, the big mistakes, the scary nights. Instead, it feels like this was preordained. "Of course I succeeded. I deserved it!"

Unfortunately, far too many bootstrappers have turned their backs on the experience that brought them where they are today. They get hooked on the money and the success and the stability. And they become arrogant.

I had a meeting last week with the president of a company that had just gone public and is now worth about half a billion dollars. A year ago, he was scraping together money to buy lunch. Two years ago, he couldn't even get a meeting. But today, he's a superconfident, superarrogant superentrepreneur who doesn't want to hear anyone else's opinion—even his staff's.

It's so easy to forget where you came from. So easy to forget that luck and pluck and a lot of help led you to success. If you follow the advice in this book, I hope it'll be a little more likely that you succeed. And I pray that after you succeed, you'll remember how you got there. And you'll take the time to help someone else make it, too.

New ways to raise bootstrap funds

Terry Mocherniak started the Lumion Corporation with $150,000 in family funds. But the company's effort to develop energy-efficient lighting controls turned out to require far more capital—even after Mocherniak, whose company is based in Wilmington, Delaware, raised another $600,000 from government grants and $1.7 million from venture capitalists. In all, Mocherniak said, they needed $750,000 to $1 million to complete the commercialization of the technology.

Those are the kinds of numbers, unfortunately, that used to bring despair to investment bankers. Mocherniak was determined not to bring any more meddling venture capitalists on board. But amounts that small are impossible to raise by a public offering, largely because of legal and accounting fees, which can easily top $500,000. Luckily for Mocherniak, however, regulators recently approved a Regulation D, or exempt stock, offering that drastically reduces costs for bootstrappers seeking funds.

To make a long story short, Mocherniak raised his $750,000 in a Regulation D offering. Costs were $60,000—not trifling, but doable. And now he has the backing to make Lumion's technology commercial.

CHAPTER EIGHT

PERSONAL
SURVIVAL

In the first Blues Brothers movie, Jake and Elwood announce that they're on a mission from God. In many ways, this same feeling is what separates the bootstrapper from everyone else.

Everybody's work is personal. But when it's your company, and you're a razor's breadth away from bankruptcy, work gets *very* personal.

It's your idea, your company, your life. And you have complete control. As a result, the disconnection that many people feel from their jobs just doesn't affect a bootstrapper. It's four o'clock on the Wednesday before Thanksgiving. Lots of employees are thinking about leaving early. A bootstrapper, on the other hand, is cursing the fact that other people are going home early, thus limiting the amount of time she has to call prospects on the phone.

As a bootstrapper, you must believe in your product. If you don't, no one else will. And you have to communicate that belief with such enthusiasm and focus that other people can't doubt your imminent success.

Virtually all of the successful bootstrappers I've ever met have this enthusiasm in common. It's one reason they're so much fun to have dinner with. The oratory of a true believer, the glint in his eyes—both suggest bootstrapping is one of the greatest uses of our DNA. Here's someone who is living his professional life to the fullest. No excuses, no distance, no safety net.

What does it take to be on this kind of mission? Not the industry you're in, that's for sure. There are missionaries in every type of bootstrapped company, from coffin sales to life insurance to software to publishing. If you're waiting for the right idea, you're looking in the wrong place.

If you're not feeling this zeal, if your job is just a job, your customers and your prospects will know it. And it will make the work you do every day much more difficult.

Remember, bootstrapping is a *process*, not an event. Can you sign up for the process? Can you put yourself on the line to the point where the business is you, where your work is at least as fun as your life?

This feeling explains why rich entrepreneurs go back and do it again. And why Bill Gates, the richest man who ever lived and the most successful bootstrapper of all time, still goes to work every day.

TIME, MONEY, AND ETHICS

At the beginning, the rush of bootstrapping will certainly cloud your judgment. You'll have trouble distinguishing between a prospect who says no and means it and someone who says no and means "I haven't heard enough yet." You may not understand the difference between a bad idea and an idea that just needs more persistence.

Unlikely successes

Homelessness and dropping out of high school aren't exactly key indicators of future success, for either bootstrappers or employees. But Lynn Carr of Hannibal, Missouri, is making both of them work for her. The founder of Twainland Cheesecake Company was herself homeless at one time. And most of her ten employees are welfare moms who didn't finish high school.

No surprise that the kitchen in which Carr turns out as many as 200 cheesecakes a week is no ordinary cookery. TV monitors constantly broadcast messages from Zig Ziglar, Brian Tracy, and other motivational speakers. Not only does the steady stream of upbeat inspiration help employees speedily season her 116 varieties of cheesecake, but it also helps them make something of themselves. Three of her employees have moved on to other jobs, and two spend part of their workday studying for high school diplomas.

EYAL BALLE

Forget the rules

It's a given among apparel and footwear retailers that any unsold items can be returned to their manufacturers for credit. But retailers who order shoes from Rebels, the Los Angeles bootstrap started by Eyal Balle, won't be giving any back. That's because this brash bootstrapper refuses to accept returns of his shoes. You buy them, you own them.

Surprisingly, given his nonconformist stance, Balle numbers no less a retail traditionalist than Nordstrom's among his stalwart clients. Refusing to accept returns makes retailers really commit to his lines before they buy them. And not having to deal with returns frees him up for the countless tasks tied to selling, lining up manufacturers, and shipping shoes. So breaking the hallowed returns rule has made Rebels stand out.

You may also have trouble drawing lines. There are three areas in which boot-strappers most often have trouble with boundaries: time, money, and ethics.

TIME

At the beginning, you have more time than money. And the temptation, since time is easier to find than money, is to use it all. To stay up until two a.m. stamping envelopes. To take a "working vacation" (what a great oxymoron!) because no one else in your office can handle things while you're gone.

You'll certainly work harder than you ever did at a "real" job. The question you need to ask yourself from the beginning is, "How hard?"

Bill Clinton and you both get exactly 24 hours in a day. No matter what you do, that's all you get. You'll need to decide how many hours you're willing to devote to your life, to sleep, and to business. And you'll have to understand tradeoffs. The president manages to run the entire free world and guard a nuclear arsenal. Surely you can do your job in less time than it takes him to do his!

Can you save $100 by pulling an all-nighter and driving that shipment to Hart-ford yourself? No doubt. But what will that cost you in terms of the productive time you could have had at the office?

And what good is a successful business if you have no husband, no kids, no family to share it with? Here's a personality indicator that never seems to fail: When an entrepreneur sets up a pattern of hours, it's never temporary. If you're used to working until eight p.m. every night, you're going to keep working until eight, even after the crisis has passed.

Many of my peers talk about what they're going to do when this crisis is over or when that financing is closed or when this client is finally satisfied. But they never do. They have an amount of time for work, and that's what they use.

So the big question, which you ought to answer right now, in writing, is: How many hours a week are you going to work? It's a finite number. Can't be more than 168 hours. So pick.

Did you do it? It takes guts to announce that you're a crazed workaholic. Even more guts to pick a sane workweek and stick with it.

One of the mantras of the successful bootstrapper is that this is life, not the dress rehearsal. You're going to be doing this for a while, so you might as well do it in a way you're proud of.

MONEY

When you start out, you'll have more money in your personal account than you will in your business. And the temptation will be to merge the two, to demonstrate your belief in the business by putting all your money there.

Guess what? Once your money's gone, it's gone forever. You've got to give up, get a job, start over. And starting over is hard.

You need to have a nest egg, a pile of money that is never touched under any circumstances. You need to be cautious about borrowing money to cover the burn rate. That money will be almost impossible to recover.

At the other end of the spectrum is the mercenary bootstrapper who won't put *any* of his own money into the venture. Bankers, investors, and employees can smell this a mile away, and it's not going to work.

Be very conscious of your attitude about personal money, personal guarantees, and loans from friends and family. Never get situation specific. It's so, so easy to say, "Just this once" or "It's a special case" or "It's worth it." Have a set of principles and stick with them.

What happens when you're facing the end of your business, no money left, great prospects but out of cash? And a banker offers you money if you'll just mortgage your house? Should you do it? Well, the time to decide is not at that moment. The time to decide was last year, when things were going fine.

A 1998 issue of *Inc.* magazine had an article on two entrepreneurs about to go public. They used their last dollar to pay the investment bankers, and then agreed to mortgage their houses to cover operating expenses. They rationalized that it was just for a little while, because after the IPO, they'd be fine.

You guessed it. The IPO got canceled. The investment bankers kept the fees. And the banks got their homes.

Situational spending—making decisions about your nest egg when the chips are down—is sure to lead to a bad outcome.

ETHICS

Speaking of principles, note this well: The ends don't justify the means. They just don't. Cheating, lying, stealing, bending the rules—none of these things is worth it, even if it means the success or failure of your business.

If you have to cheat the IRS to stay in business one more month and it works, you'll certainly do it again. You've reset your limits, and you'll test them whenever you need to.

Stew Leonard. He turned his tiny dairy store into the most profitable supermarket in America. He wrote a best-selling book and was lauded by Tom Peters and several U.S. presidents.

Unfortunately, Stew got into a bad habit early on. He cheated on his taxes. Instead of reporting all his income, he had one cash register designed to send cash straight down a slot to a safe behind his fireplace. Even when he was making millions of dollars a year, Stew was skimming off the top.

He lost his reputation and his freedom when the IRS caught him. I bet he'd give an awful lot for a chance to do it again—the right way.

As your own boss, you have plenty of opportunities to beat the system. Insurance fraud, tax fraud, contract fraud, payroll fraud—you could write a book about the many, many ways you can rip people off. Set up an offshore company and start buying things from yourself. Threaten to sue people just to extort money. You get the idea.

I got into a cab at Dulles International Airport in Dulles, Virginia, and asked the driver to take me to the offices of AOL, which is about $14 and five minutes away. He then proceeded to plot out a route that would have cost me more than $50 and taken about half an hour. Fortunately, I knew where I was going. So did he. But he had decided to take advantage of me (a stranger) to support his business and his family.

He might win in the short run. Make a few extra bucks from unsuspecting businesspeople. But he will have no foundation, no way to go straight when the time comes. Sooner or later, he'll get busted. And before that, he'll have lost his compass, and that's even more difficult to fix than a mark on his record.

Of course, it's not just your personal behavior that drives your business. It's the culture you create as well. All the people who work with you and work for you will reflect your approach to business.

If you believe in taking the last dollar off the table, in driving the hardest bargain and threatening to sue whenever possible, you can bet your organization will act the same way. Getting good work out of your vendors and your employees often calls for a more mature way of doing business.

Sorry for the lecture, but I've seen so much failure and disappointment that came

Sweat the details

It was a fine point, to be sure. Aurora Pucciarello had had a certain customer under contract for the last three years, with no problems. All Pucciarello had to do was fill out a bid sheet and return it. But she failed to do so, shuffling the bid papers into a stack until the (former) customer called to let her know the deadline had passed and Max Distribution, a $5 million Dallas logistics firm she ran as CEO, had lost the business.

Maybe returning the bid had at first seemed like a mere detail, but the deal represented 10 percent of Max's annual sales. Pucciarello used the pain to motivate her to revamp the company's bidding system to make sure no more such details would slip through the cracks. And six years later, she did finally win back the former client.

Discount strategically

Allen Harpham doesn't work cheap. At least, not without a reason. The president of Computer Consultants of Hastings, Inc., has only a few situations in which he'll charge less than the going rate for his computer skills and savvy. One of those is when a lower price may lead to a new market.

Take, for instance, the time a local hospital asked him to quote a price for installing a computer network. Harpham dropped his price to make sure he won the bid. Why? Not so much for the hospital work as for the opportunity to hook up with doctors whose offices might need consulting services. Likewise, when his local chamber of commerce wanted to set up a Web page, Harpham handled the job at a below-market rate. "It's put our name in front of other chamber members," he says. "And naturally they want to market their products on the Internet, too."

from this. Don't do anything you wouldn't be happy to tell your mother about.

Some specific things you can do about all three:

Time: Buy an answering machine. Make sure that it has a silent-answer feature. Use it. Especially if you're running a business out of your house, you'll need this. You need to make a decision: Are the additional speed and savings you'll get from being on call 24 hours a day worth the angst, loss of sleep, and hassle you'll get from living with a beeper or a phone?

Back in 1986, when I was starting out, I was working on two intense projects. One was a software deal in England (with a six-hour difference in time zones). The second was a project with a number of law firms in New York (they work crazy hours).

For months, I was always available. Working out of my home, I could easily monitor the phones and grab the answering machine if I needed to.

I was on the phone at 5 a.m. (England) and 10 p.m. (New York). And I wasn't having any fun.

The day I realized this, I hired an answering service. I also let the firms I was working with know the best times to call me.

I started working 7 a.m. to 6 p.m. Virtually no exceptions. Guess what? Business *increased.* My around-the-clock availability had done nothing to increase my sales—it had only increased my anxiety.

Twelve years later, I've managed to keep this schedule. You'll be hard pressed to find me at work on a weekend or at night. My customers don't complain, my employees don't complain, and my investors don't complain.

Work expands to fill the available space. By stating, in writing, my hours, I was able to build a life at the same time I built a business.

Pick some hours. Whatever they are. And when those hours aren't in force, don't check your voice mail, don't check your e-mail, don't carry a beeper. Just don't.

Too hard to swallow? At least set up an emergency-only system. One bootstrapper I know gives half his phone number to each of two employees. In order to call him at home, they've got to both agree to give up their data.

It's been three years, and so far no one has bothered Michael at his summer house.

Money: Do the same thing with your budgets. Allocate a certain amount of your net worth as working capital for your business. Put it in a separate account. If your business borrows money from you, charge interest. A lot of interest. Like 15 percent. Record how well your working capital account does. If you're making money lending money to yourself, go ahead and consider putting more money over there.

But be formal about it. Require two signatures on the account, for example. That way you can always blame the "no" on one of your advisers. That way you won't be so quick to dip.

The second rule: Never personally guarantee anything. Period. Once you do, you've essentially put 100 percent of your net worth into your business.

You incorporated for a reason. Stick with it. Refuse to sign a personal guarantee of any kind, for any reason. If the person offering the deal won't live with a corporate guarantee, you don't want her as a creditor. If you're borrowing money your business can't support, then don't borrow it. Grow slower.

My feeling on this is simple: If you have to guarantee loans personally to grow your business, it's not worth growing your business.

This is serious. One signature can open you up to hundreds of thousands or even

The unlikeliest bootstrap

Right behind selling ice to Siberians would be selling them pizzas, right? Not anymore. Not since Eric Shogren moved from Minneapolis to the frozen Russian province and opened a restaurant he called New York Pizza in downtown Novosibirsk. Surprisingly, Shogren lasted through his first winter—and another one since. Today there are seven New York Pizzas in the city of two million.

But take Shogren's success with a grain of caution. Even the bootstrapper admits it was not a cinch. Foreign culture, Russian regulations, and the serious problem of first teaching Siberians what pizza is made this an unlikely bootstrap of the first order. Advises Shogren, "It falls into that category of, 'Don't try this at home.'"

CYBERMEALS

Bijou bootstrap

Tim Glass was at the movies when the idea for his start-up came to him. He watched Sandra Bullock order pizza over the Internet in *The Net*, and a vision of an actual online virtual pizza parlor came to him.

It took Glass a while to work the bugs out of this system, which required orderers to input their addresses and select from a list of local participating restaurants. The order was converted to voice mail, phoned into the parlor, and confirmed by e-mail.

By 1996 a test was under way, and two years later Cybermeals had expanded beyond pizza to include 11,000 restaurants serving cuisine of every stripe. Glass had signed agreements with big-time Internet service providers like Yahoo! and America Online, and Cybermeals was the largest in a growing cadre of online meal services.

millions of dollars of exposure. Don't do it.

Ethics: Do you have a code? An ethical line you won't cross?

Would you consider buying a business from someone who kept two sets of books? I wouldn't. Someone who's willing to lie to the IRS would lie to me, too.

Nobody follows every rule all the time. And in many cases, the rules are designed to anticipate that. But at the same time, without a personal code, you have no barometer, no way to know when you've crossed the line and become a sleaze.

Earlier, in the middle of one of my ceaseless lectures, I said don't do anything you wouldn't tell your mom about. Same advice here. Tell your parents or your spouse or your kids about everything you do that's near an ethical line. Nine times out of ten, the fact that you have to say out loud what you're about to do will make you think twice about crossing your personal line.

THE IRS

Sooner or later, every bootstrapper is going to have to deal with IRS. As a general rule, the IRS isn't as flexible as most bootstrappers. It has millions of people, individuals and corporations, to deal with. So the IRS has a hard time coming up with policies that can be fairly applied to the huge variety of businesses.

The IRS has developed a culture that would rather collect a few hundred million dollars from Chrysler, given the choice, than a million dollars from three hundred different companies.

Unfortunately, as the prime engine moving our economy, bootstrappers are sitting ducks for any elected official looking to raise some money. A new tax levied on every business in this country seems like a break for the consumer, but it actually impacts huge numbers of people. Not just in money but in the hassles of dealing with the tax code.

You basically have three choices:

1. You can live underground, hoping that the IRS won't notice you.

2. You can organize your business to minimize the impact the IRS has.

3. You can file every form and wallow in it.

The first path isn't for me. For one thing, the IRS puts people in prison, which is an unhappy way to end a business career. Second, it's hard to focus and grow your business when you have to keep wondering who's watching. Third, I think that paying taxes is a privilege. And our taxes are a bargain, considering the freedom they buy us.

The second path is probably the right way to go. This path calls for an accountant who won't push you to become a big business before you're ready. It means you don't hire any employees, even yourself. Instead, you use temps or freelancers or partners.

It means you don't sell anything that would require sales tax. Instead, you use a sales agent or broker or retailer who worries about that for you. It means that you don't deduct your home office or start doing fancy things to capitalize your expenses.

Simple, straightforward bookkeeping in an LLC or subchapter S corporation. No health insurance forms, car leases, and so on. The rationale for this is simple: It will save you enough time that you can do enough new business to pay for the slightly higher taxes that may ensue as you grow.

The third strategy is what the big guys do. It's all about knowing which one of the many volumes of the IRS code is right for you. If you get good at this, you can save a ton. But of course, then you will be a tax wizard, not a bootstrapper.

Pick any path you wish. But pick. Better to deal with the IRS intentionally, and in advance, than to wait for it to find you.

CASH FLOW

Bumper sticker on a Mercedes: "Happiness is a positive cash flow." It's really that simple. If you take in more than you send out every month, sooner or later you're going to be rich.

The opposite has wiped out a whole bunch of companies, of course. When your business is growing fast, when you're focused on growth and market share, it's so easy to go negative in cash flow.

Say you sign up a customer and deliver on time, but don't get paid for 30 days. Well, that works great when you have just a few customers. But as you grow, the cash crunch starts to get serious.

The best approach? Avoiding the problem in the first place. How? Don't spend money until you get money.

Bill your clients faster than you pay your bills. Set up the terms on your big contracts to get up-front money. Create a self-priming pump that gives you more cash flow as you get bigger.

When the cash gets tight, be aware of how you're going to parcel it out. Employees and the IRS first. Vendors second. You third.

Vendors are usually understanding about cash flow if they know what to expect in advance. It's much easier for a vendor to accept delayed payment when a sale is at stake than it is later, after he's already laid out all his time and money.

By structuring every project so that it becomes cash-flow positive, you've

Down-sizing's upside

It's no secret that the best route to successful bootstrapping is an apprenticeship in the field where you want to start your business. But can corporate America actually provide you with the specific entrepreneurial skills and even capital to bootstrap yourself?

Sometimes, at least, the answer is yes, as some downsized AT&T workers have found. Starting in 1996, the phone giant decided that as part of its force-reduction plans, it would offer employees $10,000 to use as capital for forming a new business. In addition, AT&T offered courses on how to start a new business.

It's a serious offer. Barbara Miersich, a 35-year AT&T veteran, left in 1997 to start a West Orange, New Jersey, public relations consulting firm. She loves her bootstrapped existence, but she praises her ex-employer for giving her the smarts and the cash to make it on her own. About one in four downsized AT&T workers took the same offer Miersich did, including about 1,400 who received entrepreneurship training in one recent year.

From hobby to bootstrap

Matthew D'Andria and Adam Pisoni played around with computers as kids. So when the Internet revolution began, they were well positioned to turn their avocation into CyberNation, a Santa Monica, California, Web site—development bootstrap with clients like Honda and Sony. But it took more than merely setting up a fee schedule for their hobby activities.

The demands of amateurism and professionalism are quite different, D'Andria and Pisoni found. Nowadays they have to work constantly to stay up on the latest Internet technologies, while somehow maintaining the inspiration and imagination that drew them to computers in the first place. It's not easy, Pisoni says. But egging them on is the prospect of turning their one-time hobby into a big-time income stream: Three-year-old CyberNation is doing $1 million a year and growing at nearly 300 percent annually.

structured a business that is cash-flow positive.

FAST AND FEARLESS

Earlier in the book I talked about business models. One of the key competitive advantages you have as a bootstrapper is your ability to run circles around the competition.

But it's hard. It has nothing to do with your corporate structure and everything to do with your corporate attitude. Are you filled with the fear of screwing up? The fear of failing is expected, because you do have a chance of failing. But your chances of not failing aren't enhanced by your fear. Instead, they're much more likely to become something you focus on and eventually succumb to.

Many entrepreneurs have decided that without a beeper and a cell phone and around-the-clock attention to their business, they won't be able to move fast enough. I think this is nonsense. Businesses aren't slow because there isn't enough time in the day—they're slow because they're afraid.

You must be brave. Fearless. Ready to fail and eager to get up and brush yourself off. A couple of years ago at the beach, I saw a kid learning to surf. He threw himself at every wave with such abandon and joy that I knew he was going to succeed at any minute. Just a few feet away was someone waiting for exactly the right wave. He wasn't willing to fall.

Guess who got up on the board first?

You must reward yourself for bravery. Keep track of when you and your partners and your employees took smart chances. When did you launch a new initiative? How often are you willing to put yourself out of business by becoming your own biggest competitor?

Egghead Software decided to embrace the Internet. So it shut down every one of its traditional retail stores to prove to the world and to itself that Egghead was serious about the change. Compare this to IBM, which says it's serious about e-commerce. Yet IBM continues to cripple everything it does online because it's not willing to threaten the 11 business units that currently sell through salespeople and retailers.

How often do you try a radically new marketing technique or experiment with a risky pricing strategy? Have you ever tried storming out of a sales meeting that wasn't going well, just to see what would happen? What have you got to lose?

People can tell when you're fearless. They can see it in your eyes and smell it when you walk into the room. And the fearless bootstrapper quickly discovers that she has earned the respect—and the business—of many of the people she works with.

Your clients are afraid. They don't want to take risks, they don't want to rock the boat, they don't want to move fast. If you can give them a safe, reliable way to leverage your fearlessness, you've added a competitive weapon to your marketing arsenal.

The second half of fearlessness and bravery is speed. It takes guts to be fast, because speed eliminates groupthink. You'll certainly offend people by being fast. You can't arrange every committee meeting, get every approval, complete every test cycle when you're fast.

One direct marketing company I've worked with takes more than 15 months to go from a new product idea to a mailer selling that product to a large audience. Fifteen months for a process that could have been accomplished in 30 days.

The difference? Meetings. Approvals. Excess baggage slowing the process down in a way explicitly designed so that no one in the company could be held responsible for what happened. When something failed, it wasn't a problem because, after all, everyone had approved it.

By the way, this company, once the largest in its industry, is nearly bankrupt. It got killed by faster companies willing to take risks.

YOUR MOTTO

Earlier, I talked about developing a positioning statement for your company. About why people won't understand who you are or what you're selling unless you can capture the essence of it in 12 words or fewer.

All of the great brands in this country have clearly defined positions in the marketplace. Their makers can clearly and succinctly describe exactly where the brands fit in their prospect's mental landscape. And this position gets stronger over time.

But do you have a positioning statement? A personal motto for who you are and what you bring to work every day? When people talk about you, what do they say?

When you don't have a boss, it's so easy to vacillate, to cut corners, to indulge yourself. Having a motto keeps you in line. Having a motto makes it easy for you to measure yourself against the self you'd like to be.

Do you have a mentor? What's her motto? The best people, the most effective people, the managers who attract great employees, run profitable businesses, and satisfy their investors almost always have mottoes.

BEYOND
BOOTSTRAPPING

Someday, you may discover that your business has finally made it. Persistence, hard work, focus, and energy usually pay off. And you'll find that you're making money every month and that new opportunities continue to present themselves.

What do you do now? How do you grow your business to serve all the people who want your products? Should you grow it? Where will you find the money?

Here's the good news and the bad news: You're in a great spot. You've reached the goal that most bootstrappers set for themselves. You've succeeded. You have a job, a career, a business, and a life. Congratulations! The bad news is that it's not going to get much better than this, not for a long time.

Bootstrapping is a rush. It's an exciting adventure that pushes you and challenges you to do better and better every day. And it's filled with rewards. But once you reach a certain level of achievement, you may find that the rewards don't seem as rewarding, that the excitement isn't as exciting.

If you start feeling a sense of ennui closing in, you're not alone. Countless entrepreneurs have found that success is their worst enemy. "Now that I've climbed this mountain, where's the next one?"

And here's my surprising advice: Think long and hard about growing. Think long and hard about what talents got you this far, and which talents you're going to need moving forward.

You've got three options once you reach success: You can keep on keeping on. Grow very slowly. Make money. Do great work. Or you can sell your business and start a new one. Or you can get some money from an angel or a venture capitalist or a bank and really grow your business.

The most-noticed companies choose the third path. Companies like Starbucks and Yahoo! and Microsoft and Del Monte and on and on and on.

I'm going to be bold and hypothesize that the skills most entrepreneurs use to bootstrap are almost useless when it comes to building a successful large company. Sooner or later, virtually all of the company founders are forced out of or choose to leave their own companies. Bill Gates is the exception. For every supertalented billionaire entrepreneur, there are dozens of bootstrappers who were smart enough to bail out before their board fired them.

To grow your business to the next level, you'll almost always need someone else's money. And the day you take someone else's money, the company ceases to be yours alone. Sure, you can maintain control of the board and have an ironclad contract. But once that money is coursing through your company's veins, you owe someone. And if you choose to act on your own behalf instead of your investors', you'll discover that sources of money dry up instantly.

You make a deal when you raise money. In exchange for the money, you agree to transform your company fundamentally—from a bootstrapped operation to one that will be bigger than you, bigger than your personal vision and energy. It becomes an independent third party, a living, breathing entity.

Don't take your business to the next level because *Inc.* magazine makes it look glamorous. And don't do it because you think your life and your company will stay the same, but bigger. Do it because you want to transform yourself as well, because you want to grow and change and become a different kind of entrepreneur and manager.

It's really hard. Harder than most of us who made the switch could ever imagine. Michael Dell remembers hand-assembling computers in his college dorm. Now he runs a multibillion-dollar public company, the world's single largest seller of computers by direct response.

Is his life better? Not in every way, certainly. And the nostalgia for the freedom and control he had in those days must certainly gnaw at him when he walks into a tough board meeting. But the experiences he's had, the things he's learned more than make up for it (most of the time!).

If you're a true bootstrapper, an entrepreneur who can't resist a blank sheet of paper and a new idea, you need to think really long and hard about the second option—selling your company and starting over.

Sell your company for enough money to fall back on. Buy yourself a new Miata, take a great vacation, and then put the rest in the bank. And then, without using your nest egg, start again with no money. Life's a journey—enjoy the ride.

If that challenge sounds like the perfect path for you, go for it. Resist the pressure to be Michael Dell or Steve Jobs or Bill Gates. Be you.

On the other hand, if you really want to move to a different level, here are five things to keep in mind:

1. *Your funded business must scale*. Scaling means growth as a direct result of further investment. Cash needs to be fairly directly related to growth. If your business needs other things to grow—unique talent, fundamental changes in market conditions, a technology break-through—you need to think about exactly where you're going to raise this money.

Banks don't invest with failure in mind. They want to lend money to entrepreneurs with a guaranteed scalable plan. A venture capitalist, on the other hand, focuses on those risks and is far more likely to invest in the face of them.

But understand that a venture capitalist earns a return of five or ten times that of a bank. And be sure you're ready to outline every one of the risks you face in scaling your business before you talk to tany investors.

2. *Your funded business must have a structure*. You can't have everyone reporting to you, nor can you make all the decisions. You can't make your own policy decisions on the fly, and you need an employee hand-book and a company law firm.

Most important, you need staff who are empowered to make significant business decisions without you. You must be prepared to cede significant amounts of con-trol in your scaled business. Once you pass 40 or 50 employees, your company pretty much has to run itself—your job is about working the outside world, not, unfortunately, about inventing the next product line.

3. *There are a million ways to screw up, but just a few ways to succeed*. As you become bigger, the wide-open spaces you faced as a solo bootstrap-per get smaller. Your organization will become unwieldy compared to the sprightly little group you shepherded during the early days.

That means you have to make big decisions early—never at the last minute. And you have turn down business that's off the topic.

4. *There will be competition.* And you have to have a plan for dealing with that competition. A bootstrapper doesn't need all the business— just enough to be happy. But a funded business needs to be focused on maximizing market share.

5. *You need an exit strategy.* The minute your company takes someone else's money, he's going to start watching where you take that money. Which means that if you're planning to extract a significant amount of money from your business, you've got to figure out how to replace that money for you and your investors. And that means ultimately selling the company or going public.

Planning for and accepting that eventuality is best done earlier, not later.

I'm delighted that I made the transition. My investors have been terrific. They're smart and helpful and patient and honest—all you can ask for. The journey has had thousands of pitfalls, and I've learned a lot as I've grown a real company. I now have employees I've never really met, decisions that are made without me, and long-term plans far outside my usual realm of consciousness. It's a journey many people don't get to go on, and if you're up for it, I heartily recommend it.

LEARNING
THE LINGO

Do you really know the language that other businesspeople throw around? Here's some essential bootstrapper vocabulary.

Accrual: In this common accounting method, accountants don't count cash as cash. They count a sale as being made when the work is done, not when the money comes in.

Allowable: How much money a marketer is willing to spend to get one more sale. American Express, for example, has an allowable of $150 for one new cardmember sign-up.

Amortized: Accountants often spread over time a company's expense of purchasing an item. The company pays all at once, but slowly deducts the cost from profits.

Brand Equity: The momentum a brand has in the eyes of consumers.

Brand Recognition: A survey that determines how many people recognize a brand either with or without prompting.

BRC: Business reply card. Or postcard you can mail back without a stamp.

Buck Slip: A three-inch by six-inch slip of paper (about the size of a dollar bill) inserted in a direct-mail piece.

Burn Rate: How much it costs you to run your business every month, not counting income or marginal expenses.

Capitalized Expenses: Before you can amortize expenses, you put them in a special category and capitalize them.

Cash Basis: Bootstrappers often keep track of business based on when the cash comes in. A good idea!

Cash Flow: How much money goes into or out of your business every month.

Clickthrough: On the Internet, when someone clicks on your banner, that's a clickthrough.

Closing: The art of getting a customer to overcome her fear and buy something.

Compliance: Following federal and state regulations when doing business.

Co-op: Local advertising that is partially paid for by the manufacturer of the product. For example, when you see books in a Barnes & Noble ad, the ads were paid for by the publisher, not B&N.

CPM: Cost per thousand is the unit of measurement among advertisers. How much money will it take to reach 1,000 people?

Dating: Not paying your bills exactly on time. Paying net 30-day bills 15 days late is 45-day dating.

Earnings per Share: The income of the company divided by the number of shares.

EGD: Environmental graphic design is the art of building signs and other elements that make your office or store look great.

Fixed Cost: Any cost you have, no matter how good or bad business is.

Focus Group: A bunch of strangers sitting in a room, behind one-way glass, talking about a new product you've invented. Do not treat the comments as fact. This approach isn't scientific. It's just to raise questions, not give you answers.

Frequency: How often one person sees a particular ad.

FSI: A free standing insert is that colorful newspaper portion filled with coupons.

Gross Margin: The difference between the price you sell something for and what it costs you to make (not counting your overhead). (Net revenue minus marginal cost.)

Gross Rating Points: The method used for determining how many people a TV commercial reaches.

Gross Revenue: The total amount of money you receive for products you sell.

Growth Share Matrix: A company with multiple products and businesses might find that some are dogs (low market share, low growth), some are stars (high market share, high growth), some are cash cows (high market share, low growth), and some are problem children (low market share, high growth). The goal, of course, is to use the cash cows to fund the problem children.

Impressions: When one ad reaches one person, that's an impression. You get two impressions when the same ad reaches the same person twice.

Inbound Telemarketing: An 800 number with a campaign that gets people to call you, with operators standing by. Outbound telemarketing is when the operators call you (at home during dinner, of course).

Incremental Cost: The difference between one item's costs and another's. For example, the incremental cost to convert a Nike track shoe into a snow boot is $2.

Inventory Turn: How many times each year one product on the shelf will sell.

IPO: An initial public offering is the first time a company sells stock to the public.

Key Grip: A trick question! This person does something at the movies.

LBO: A leveraged buyout, in which you use the company you are buying as collateral when borrowing the money to buy the company.

List Broker: Like a travel agent for mailing lists. The broker charges nothing, takes a commission from the owner of the list, and can rent you just about any mailing list in the world.

Marginal Cost: The cost of making just one more widget. It doesn't include overhead.

Market Share: Percentage of all sales in your defined market that you acquire.

MDF: Market development funds are slush funds that marketers use to make particular areas of the county sell more product. A great source for money!

MIS: Management information systems, a fancy word for computers. In this as in most things, you get what you pay for.

Net Revenue: Gross revenue minus commissions.

Net 30: The amount you have to pay on an invoice if you pay within 30 days.

Obligating Question: The most important moment in selling. "Mr. Prospect, if I understand you correctly, if our product can do x, y, and z, are you prepared to buy it today?" It's the best way to figure out who's serious and who's just looking.

Onpack Promotion: A consumer promotion, such as a rebate coupon, that's actually glued to the outside of the box.

Open to Buy: Buyers at retail stores have a budget to spend every month in acquiring products. This is money they must spend.

Options: The right to buy shares in a company at a later date, usually for a fixed price.

Positioning: A product occupies a position in the consumer's brain or it disappears. There is no room for others. Your product can be cheapest or fastest or coolest, but you must create a unique spot for it.

Product Life Cycle: After products are launched, they thrive, then wither and die, and must be replaced by others.

Profit: What's left after expenses, overhead, and taxes.

Prospecting: The science of turning strangers into people legitimately interested in your product.

Reach: The number of different people who see an ad.

Retention Program: A way to get consumers to stay, not switch.

Saliency: Similar to brand recognition, it's the number of people who, unaided, can identify a particular brand as a leader.

Self-liquidating Premium: A promotion to consumers in which the amount the consumer pays for "postage and handling" equals or exceeds the cost of buying the item in the first place.

Shelf Space: A commodity often resold by retailers. The more shelf space, the more sales.

Shelving Allowance: A nice word for the money paid by manufacturers to get their products on the shelves.

Short-term Liability: Money your company owes in the next few months.

Spiff: A legal payment made by a manufacturer to a retail salesperson for selling his product instead of someone else's.

TQM: Total Quality Management, a way of getting your quality to go up at the same time your costs go down.

UPC: The Universal Product Code is that little striped gizmo on grocery items that tells computers exactly what was sold.

Variable Cost: Any cost that changes when you make more or fewer widgets.

Warrants: The right to receive shares in a company at a later date, usually for free.

RESOURCES

Books

Bootstrappers' Success Secrets. Kimberly Stansell (Career Press, 1997).

The Business Planning Guide, 8th ed. David H. Bangs, Jr. (Upstart Publishing, 1998).

The Entrepreneur Magazine Small Business Advisor. (John Wiley & Sons, 1995).

Franchising 101. ASBDC, Edited by Ann Dugan (Upstart Publishing, 1998).

Guerrilla Financing. Bruce Jan Blechman and Jay Conrad Levinson (Houghton Mifflin, 1992).

Guerrilla Marketing for the Home-Based Business. Jay Conrad Levinson and Seth Godin (Houghton Mifflin, 1995).

The Guerrilla Marketing Handbook. Jay Levinson and Seth Godin (Houghton Mifflin, 1995).

How to Buy a Great Business with No Cash Down. Arnold S. Goldstein (John Wiley & Sons, 1991).

How to Form Your Own Corporation without a Lawyer for under $75.00. Ted Nicholas (Upstart Publishing, 1996).

How to Incorporate: A Handbook for Entrepreneurs and Professionals. Michael R. Diamond and Julie L. Williams (John Wiley & Sons, 1996).

How to Start, Finance, and Manage Your Own Small Business. Joseph R. Mancuso (Fireside, 1992).

If You're Clueless about Starting Your Own Business and Want to Know More. Seth Godin (Upstart Publishing, 1998).

Insuring Your Business: What You Need to Know to Get the Best Insurance Coverage for Your Business. Sean Mooney (Insurance Information Institute, 1991).

The Legal Guide for Starting and Running a Small Business. Fred S. Steingold (Nolo Press, 1997).

Mancuso's Small Business Resource Guide. Joseph R. Mancuso (Sourcebooks, 1996).

Positioning. Al Ries and Jack Trout (Warner Books, 1993).

SBA Loans: A Step-by-Step Guide. Patrick D. O'Hara (John Wiley & Sons, 1994).

The Small Business Start-Up Guide. Hal Root and Steve Koenig (Sourcebooks Trade, 1994).

The Start-Up Guide, 3rd ed. David H. Bangs, Jr. (Upstart Publishing, 1998).

Succeeding in Small Business: The 101 Toughest Problems and How to Solve Them. Jane Applegate (Plume, 1992).

Successful Telemarketing. Bob Stone and John Wyman (NTC Publishing, 1993).

Tax Savvy for Small Business: Year-Round Tax Advice for Small Business. Frederick W. Daily (Nolo Press, 1997).

The Upstart Small Business Legal Guide. Robert Friedman (Upstart Publishing, 1998).

Working from Home: Everything You Need to Know about Living and Working under the Same Roof. Paul Edwards and Sarah Edwards (Putnam Publishing Group, 1994).

Magazines, Newspapers, and Other Publications

BusinessWeek, 1221 Avenue of the Americas, New York, NY 10020, 800-635-1200, $49.95/yr., weekly.

Entrepreneur, PO Box 50368, Boulder, CO 80321, 800-274-6229, $19.97/yr., monthly.

Family Business Magazine, 229 South 18th St., Rittenhouse Square, Philadelphia, PA 19103, 215-567-3200, free, quarterly.

Fast Company, 450 West 33rd Street, 11th floor, New York, NY, 10001, 800-688-1545, $19.75/yr., 10 issues.

Forbes, 60 Fifth Ave., New York, NY 10011, 800-888-9896, $57/yr., biweekly.

Fortune, PO Box 60001, Tampa, FL 33660, 800-621-8000, $57/yr., biweekly.

Inc., PO Box 54129, Boulder, CO 80323, 800-234-0999, $19/yr., 18 issues.

Nation's Business, US Chamber of Commerce Center for Small Business, 1615 H St. NW, Washington, DC 20062, 202-463-5503, $22/yr., monthly.

New York Times, PO Box 2047, South Hackensack, NJ 07606, 800-631-2500, $374.40/yr., daily.

Wall Street Journal, 200 Liberty St., New York, NY 10281, 800-568-7625, $175.00/yr., daily.

Newsletters

Bootstrappin' Entrepreneur, c/o Kimberly Stansell, Suite 306-BSS, 6308 West 89th St., Los Angeles, CA 90045, single copy $8 outside CA or $8.60 in CA. Or send self-addressed, stamped envelope for more information.

Family Business Advisor, PO Box 4356, Marietta, GA 30061, 770-425-6673, $139/yr., monthly.

Small Business Bulletin, Small Business Service Bureau, 554 Main St., Worcester, MA 01608, 508-756-3513, free to members, quarterly.

Organizations

Active Corps of Executives (ACE), Small Business Administration, 409 3rd St. SW, Washington, DC 20416, 800-827-5722.

American Bankers Association, 1120 Connecticut Ave. NW, Washington, DC 20036, 202-663-5000.

American Management Association (AMA), 1601 Broadway, New York, NY 10019, 212-586-8100.

Association of Small Business Development Centers, 1313 Farnum, Ste. 132, Omaha, NE 68182, 402-595-2387.

Bankers Systems, PO Box 1457, St. Cloud, MN 56302, 612-251-3060.

Center for Family Business, PO Box 24268, Cleveland, OH 44124, 440-442-0800.

Ewing Marion Kauffman Foundation, PO Box 8480, 9300 Ward Parkway, Kansas City, MO 64114, 816-966-4000.

Federal Trade Commission, Sixth and Pennsylvania Ave. NW, Washington, DC 20580, 202-326-3175.

General Services Administration, 1800 F St. NW, Washington, DC 20405, 202-501-1231.

Independent Bankers Association, PO Box 267, 1168 South Main St., Sauk Center, MN 56378, 612-352-6546.

Institute of Management Consultants, 521 Fifth Ave., 35th floor, New York, NY 10175, 800-221-2557.

National Association of Home-Based Businesses, PO Box 362, 10451 Mill Run Circle, Ste. 400, Owings Mills, MD 21117, 410-363-3698.

National Association of Investment Companies (NAIC), 1111 14th St. NW, Ste. 700, Washington, DC 20005, 202-289-4336.

National Association for the Self-Employed (NASE), PO Box 612067, DFW Airport, TX 75261, 800-232-6273.

National Association of Small Business Investment Companies (NASBIC), 1199 North Fairfax St., Ste. 200, Alexandria, VA 22314, 703-351-5269.

National Association of State Development Agencies, 750 First St., Ste. 710, Washington, DC 20002, 202-898-1302.

National Federation of Independent Business, Capitol Gallery East, Ste. 700, 600 Maryland Ave. SW, Washington, DC 20024, 202-554-9000.

National Small Business United, 1156 15th St. NW, Ste. 710, Washington, DC 20005, 202-293-8830.

National Venture Capital Association, 1655 North Fort Myer Drive, Ste. 700, Arlington, VA 22209, 703-351-5269.

Open University, 255 South Orange Ave., Orlando, FL, 32801, 407-649-8488.

Procurement Automated Source System, Small Business Administration, 409 3rd St. SW, Washington, DC 20416, 202-205-6469.

Service Corps of Retired Executives (SCORE), Small Business Administration, 409 Third St. SW, Washington, DC 20416, 800-827-5722.

Sheshunoff Information Services, One Texas Center, 505 Barton Springs Rd., Ste. 1200, Austin, TX 78704, 512-472-2244.

Small Business Administration, 409 Third St., Suite 4000 SW, Washington, DC 20416, 800-827-5722.

Small Business Service Bureau, 554 Main St., Worcester, MA 01608, 508-756-3513.

US Chamber of Commerce Center for Small Business, 1615 H St. NW, Washington, DC 20062, 202-463-5503.

Veribank, PO Box 461, Wakefield, MA 01880, 781-245-8370.

Online

American Express: http://www.americanexpress.com

America's Business Funding Directory: http://www.businessfinance.com/search.htm
Matches businesses searching for capital with lending institutions or investors. Includes a guide designed to increase your chances of getting funding, information about small business centers and venture capital clubs, and a 30-day online classified-ad service.

Business Filings Incorporated: http://wwwbizfilings.com/incinfo.htm
For low-cost, online incorporating and formation of limited liability companies, plus trademark search and registration services.

BusinessWeek Online: http://www.businessweek.com

Entrepreneur Magazine Online: http://www.entrepreneurmag.com

Fast Company Web Site: http://www.fastcompany.com

Home Office Computing Online: America Online Keywords: HOC, SoHo

Inc. Magazine Online: America Online Keyword: Inc.

Internal Revenue Service Business Taxpayer Info:
http://www.irs.ustreas.gov/plain/search/sitetree.html

SBA Online: http://www.sbaonline.sba.gov

The Small Business Advisor: http://www.isquare.com
For online advice on starting and running a small business. Includes information on business insurance, taxes, books, and US government procurement, as well as links to other business-related sites.

The Small Business Resource Center: http://www.webcom.com/seaquest/sbrc/welcome.html
For free reports on choosing, starting, and running a small business; a catalog of books, tapes, and courses; and links to other small business resources.

US Business Advisor: http://www.business.gov/index.html
Provides businesses with access to federal government information and services, including step-by-step guides, tools, answers to common questions, regulations, news, and links to other online resources.

US Chamber of Commerce Center for Small Business: http://www.uschamber.org

Venture Capital World Online: http://www.vcworld.com
For a direct database link between investors searching for opportunities and entrepreneurs looking for venture capital.

VirtualBusiness.Net: http://www.virtualbusiness.net/index.html#4
For frequently updated small business information, resources, and services, including VirtualBusiness.News, a weekly electronic newsletter with how-tos and feature articles; discussion forum; library with access to articles on business; and links to other online business resources.

http://www.babson.edu/entrep/res.html#erc2
Information about a study conducted by Reynolds Entrepreneurial Research Consortium—a cooperative effort of almost 100 small-business researchers from 20 institutions—that examines start-ups and how they grow.

Business Forms Resources

The Complete Book of Small Business Legal Forms. Daniel Sitarz (Nova Publishing, 1996).

Court TV Legal Help: http://www.courttv.com/legalhelp/business

INDEX